**CELEBRATION
OF HAND-HOOKED
RUGS 26**
2016 Edition

Editor
Debra Smith

Coordinator
Sandy Oravec

Designer
CW Design Solutions, Inc.

Advertising Director
Keith Kousins

Customer Service
Publisher's Service Associates
U.S. (877) 297-0965
Canada (866) 375-8626

Publisher
Ampry Publishing, LLC

*Rug photographs provided by the artists
unless otherwise noted.*

Rug Hooking (ISSN 1045-4373) is
published five times a year in Jan./
Feb., March/April/May, June/July/
Aug.,Sept./Oct., and Nov./Dec. by
Ampry Publishing, LLC, 3400 Dundee
Road, Suite 220, Northbrook, IL 60062.
Celebration of Hand-Hooked Rugs
is published annually. Contents

A Publication of

R·U·G
HOOKING

P.O. Box 388
Shermans Dale, PA 17090

www.rughookingmagazine.com
rughook@amprycp.com

ISBN-978-1-945550-01-0

Printed in U.S.A.

WELCOME TC

What

Ask us what's new with *Celebration of Hand-Hooked Rugs 26*, and
we're going to invite you to pour yourself a cup of coffee or tea and get
comfortable—we've got a lot to say!
First, let's talk about roots and wings.

More than a quarter-century ago, Stackpole Books had the vision of taking the
highly respected *News and Views*, by Joan Moshimer, and nurturing it into one of
the publisher's flagship publications, **Rug Hooking** magazine—deep and wonderful
roots that led to creation of the annual *Celebration of Hand-Hooked Rugs*, one of
the premier juried presentations in the rug-hooking world.

This year, Ampry Publishing has given the publication wings: an image-rich
website with many opportunities to respond to articles and artists, a new entry
site and process for *Celebration*, and a fresh vision for magazines and books in the
complex world of publishing today.

Now let's talk about that 26.

You've been used to seeing Roman numerals in the *Celebration* title, but last
year we determined that XXV—our 25th anniversary—would be a good time to
make a change. We wanted to make each issue more readily identifiable, to fit the
style of the diverse and contemporary community that rug hooking has become.

Finally, and most important, this issue!

Creativity is the word in rug hooking these days. Of the 70 rugs in this edition,
nearly half are original designs. And even in the traditional or adapted designs, you
will see an incredible energy in color choices and in hooking and finishing techniques. And note the yarn rugs this year! We think we're seeing more of those, but
time will tell.

The rug hooking community—with its artists, teachers, dyers, wool mills,
pattern designers, and tool makers—is a thriving and happy place, and we are so
grateful to be part of it.

Congratulations to the artists of *Celebration 26*! Enjoy this year's amazing work.
And have a pencil ready. You're going to want to take notes!

ON THE COVER: *Greta Garbo, hooked by Susan J. Baker, 2014. See page 93 for the
story of this stunning rug.*

Table of Contents

RUGS BASED ON ADAPTATIONS

RUGS BASED ON PRIMITIVE DESIGNS

HONORABLE MENTIONS

Meet the Judges

Not long after we gave this year's judges access to the Celebration website for judging, we got our first email: "Wow!"

And that was soon echoed by the other three.

Their enthusiasm is typical of the wonderful teachers who make rug hooking the vibrant and supportive community that it is.

We are so grateful to this year's judges, who committed a serious block of time to carefully review multiple images of each and every entry. You know these artists and teachers from workshops, retreats, and exhibitions, so you can appreciate the value of the hours they donate in order to bring you this notable annual selection of amazing textile art in the medium of rug hooking.

Thank you—Gene, Kris, Roslyn, and Wanda! We are so grateful for your participation!

WANDA KERR

Wanda Kerr is the ringmaster of the online studio and magazine *The Welcome Mat*, where she delivers daily hooking and dyeing inspiration, plus instruction to farflung rug hookers. She has an online rug school where you can wander the halls freely or sign up for classes in The Wandaway Studio. Wanda is an award-winning hooking artist with a unique style and passion for color. The thing she loves best about rug hooking is that so many wonderful avenues are still unexplored for creativity and fun. She revels in the glorious realm of possibilities. You can read her *Rug Hooking* magazine column, "Colors to Dye For," in every issue. Learn more about her various offerings, including Majic Carpet Dyes, at *www.wandaworks.ca*.

KRIS MILLER

Kris Miller is a self-taught, award-winning rug hooker who specializes in primitive designs with an emphasis on textured wool and wide cuts (#8 and above). Roving, sheep curls, paisleys, novelty yarns, and hosiery are also some of her favorite hooking materials. She is the owner of Spruce Ridge Studios in Howell, Michigan. Several of her original designs have been featured as pattern inserts in *Rug Hooking* magazine and in the books *Projects For Primitive Rug Hookers*, *Pattern Designs for Rug Hookers*, and *Finishing Hooked Rugs*. Her work was selected for three editions of *Early American Life's Directory of Traditional American Crafts*. The author of *Introduction to Rug Hooking* (2015), Kris has taught at workshops and rug camps across the United States and England. Learn more at *www.spruceridgestudios.com*.

ROSLYN LOGSDON

Roslyn Logsdon studied art in college and started out as a painter while working as a junior high school teacher. She discovered rug hooking after moving from New York City to the Washington, D.C. area and has never looked back. Her pictorial hookings feature people at cafés, two or three people conversing, or large groups of people. Her architectural designs include many variations on gothic arches. Her writings and hookings have been featured in *Rug Hooking* magazine and in a variety of books, including her own **Roslyn Logsdon: People and Places.** She teaches classes and workshops at her studio in the Montpelier Arts Center in Laurel, Maryland. Her classes stress self-expression and creativity, and her workshops explore various themes, among them monochromatics, views through windows, Japanese design, the use of unusual materials, and people and places. Learn more at *roslynlogsdon.net*.

GENE SHEPHERD

Gene Shepherd has been experimenting with all forms of hooked and prodded rug making since 1998. He is the author of *The Rug Hooker's Bible* (2005), *Prodded Hooking for a Three Dimensional Effect* (2008) and *Prepared to Dye* (2013). Gene began blogging in 2007 and has written over 3,000 blog posts about rug hooking and related topics. He has also written and filmed over 120 instructional videos on various aspects of rug hooking and dyeing. Director of Cambria Pines Rug Camp since 2001, Gene teaches private and group classes in his home studio in Anaheim, California. He also travels extensively, teaching and lecturing at rug camps, workshops, and other events. He has a passion for introducing rug hooking to multi-ethnic children and adults and has traveled to Russia, England, Canada, and Australia to teach this art form. Learn more at *www.geneshepherd.com*.

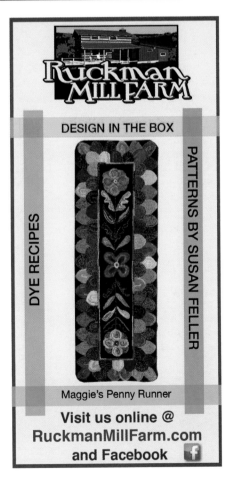

A Dream of Sailing

I spent many, many weekends sailing on the Columbia River with my parents in my youth and early adult years. It was a full sensory experience: brisk wind, waves, hot sun, cold rain, and vistas of Mt. Hood, fir trees, birds, and color everywhere. I still regularly have sailing dreams and, as is common with dreams, the normal laws of physics and the arrangement of the world don't apply.

This theme occurred to me when I was taking a design class at Puget Sound Rug School in March 2015 from Marianne Wise. It was an excellent class. At the same time I had been "cross training" by learning to draw Zentangles®. Breaking down motifs into simple lines improved my drawing skills, and the process gave me a chance to practice composition. A lot of geometric motifs were used, as well. This influenced the way I developed the motifs on my pattern when I began hooking.

I began hooking this rug at Friends by the Sea Rug Camp at Rockaway Beach, Oregon. I brought a selection of greens, blues, and yellows with me to begin the rug. The geometric shapes worked well for the triangles representing trees, the round sun, and the round turquoise-and-blue shape representing water and Earth. I found a beautiful piece of purple dip dye for the mountain (which in no way looks like Mt. Hood).

As I worked on these things, I was mulling over what to do about the background. My favorite approach to color planning a rug is to select a color palette that suits the mood of the piece I am going to hook, and then to play with the color on each motif as I begin to work on it. I usually have an idea of where I want to put the darkest dark and the lightest light on the rug and where the focal point is, of course, but there is generally no firm plan for the specific colors. This keeps it more entertaining for me.

As I thought about the background for this rug, I was remembering some of the abstract paintings I had found on Pinterest in which I loved the flow of color. I wanted to do that in this piece, but I was unable to envision swathes of color in a way that wouldn't interfere with the graphics of sails, trees, mountain, and water. So the inch-mat technique came to mind. I started with the lightest yellowish sun colors in the upper right-hand corner and the darkest purples in the lower left corner. I used 10 to 12 variations of hue for each of the main color families in the rug. When blending two different color families, I pulled a bit of similar value from each pile of hue, such as purple and blue, and mixed them in several one-inch squares. Gradually an area became more blue than purple, then more green than blue.

The biggest problem I had with this rug was getting that boat sailing up out of the purple to look less like a banana and more like a boat close-hauled to the wind. If viewers are mystified, I'm not surprised. For me, that boat sailing out of the purple might be a message, or an inspiration, or a bit of magic rising out of the deep unconscious to find expression in the light . . . or maybe just a banana.

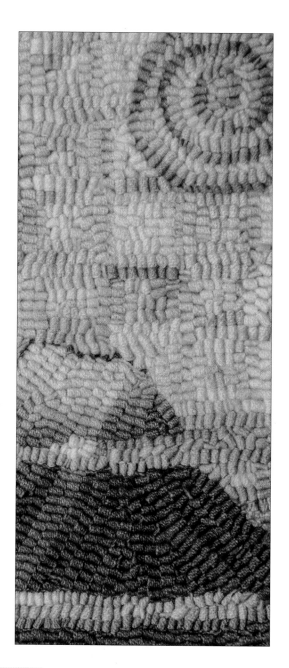

Lynne D. Powell
Portland, Oregon

Lynne started rug hooking in 1993 after she discovered the Portland Rug Hooking Guild at a Gathering of the Guilds. Her future friends loaned her a frame, gave her a small bag of wool and a simple pattern, and sold her a hook for $4.50. She is a certified McGown Teacher and a member of ATHA. This is her third rug to be chosen for Celebration.

In The Judges' Eyes

Love this interpretation! Engaging background study; excellent color work, dynamic design; your eyes move/sail around the piece.

A Dream of Sailing, 20" x 29", #4- and 5-cut hand-dyed and as-is wool on linen.
Designed and hooked by Lynne D. Powell, Portland, Oregon, 2015. OWEN CAREY PHOTOGRAPHY

A Shih Tzu's First Snow

My absolute craziness for my tiny Shih Tzu, Audrey, named after Audrey Hepburn, and my love for rug hooking just about demanded I do a hooking of her. I have photos in which she is better groomed and looks more elegant, but this photo promised to be more fun to hook. This was Audrey's first snow and, being an experienced dog owner, I knew to have my camera ready. As Audrey got covered with the cold white stuff, she looked up at me and I snapped the picture.

Six years later I was ready to hook this portrait of her in her naturally messy state. I'm really trying to be more adventurous in my hooking, and this photo was perfect. Since Audrey is black and white and I love

bright colors, experimenting on my computer helped me to decide where to use color.

Other than the white, which I bought new, the rest of the wool in this piece was cut strips left over from various other projects. For instance, I had dyed the blues, which were essential to this hooking, for my *Facescape* hooking (*Celebration XXIV*). Having white as the only large block of color in this hooking made it possible to use various shades of leftover blues and browns in the separated strands of the dog's fur. The white used was the whitest I could find; the black is not black at all, but instead, a crisp navy blue, which I find hooks up darker and looks more alive than black.

After agonizing over where to begin

hooking that tangle of hair, I finally jumped in and began with the topknot that had fallen in front of Audrey's eyes. Then I hooked her eyes, mouth, and nose—and gradually snuck up on everything else. I worked on the most noticeable locks of hair first and filled in between them, remembering to add snow here and there, especially around the eyes, so they wouldn't get lost in the dark fur. I hooked the white areas last to keep them clean while I was hooking the darker parts.

A Shih Tzu's First Snow won Grand Champion and best in show at my county fair, and was shown in March at The Columbia Art Center in Maryland. It now hangs over a staircase in our home, where my husband and I can enjoy it every day.

A Shih Tzu's First Snow, 31" x 28½", #3-cut wool on linen.
Designed and hooked by Carol Koerner, Bethesda, Maryland, 2015.

Carol Koerner
Bethesda, Maryland

This is the 12th time Carol's work has appeared in Celebration. She's been hooking for 20 years and does her own designing, color planning, and dyeing. Vivid colors with strong contrasts are her style. Some other interests are photography and gardening.

Love the reduction of this scene to essential elements of dog and snow; very original design. Spectacular use of color and shade to draw the eye; love how the dog fades into the snow and the terrific unexplained right-hand corner.

Across from the Art Gallery of Ontario

Inspiration: I really do like Toronto. When I was 18, I moved to Toronto to go to school. Toronto's not my hometown but my home by choice. Toronto is about neighborhoods. Toronto's big, but you can choose one little neighborhood and make it home.

My friend Judy and I visited the haunts of our youth. We had lived just around the corner from the Art Gallery of Ontario. Later my husband and I lived just around a different corner from the Art Gallery. We gravitated towards this neighbohood because of the heritage houses. These are beautiful houses built in the Queen-Anne-Revival style. Because these Victorian houses were listed as heritage properties, they have stayed much the same, in contrast to the big changes at the Art Gallery of Ontario and my alma mater, the Ontario College of Art.

The streetcar is also an important part of Toronto's heritage. A streetcar has been running past this house since the nineteenth century. So the streetcar route is heritage even if the streetcar is a newish model. I hooked this rug from a photo that I took in 2005. I prefer the streetcar to other modes of transit. It is powered by an electric overhead cable and runs on tracks. You glide along, quietly and smoothly, and with a view, because you are just a little higher than other vehicles on the street.

Process: I used so many textured wools that I thought about calling this rug, *Toronto Textures.* I used a lot of Dorr's New England Ombre stripes. I used a rust-colored one for the brick, and a green one for the reflections in the streetcar window. There are windows on both sides of the streetcar, so

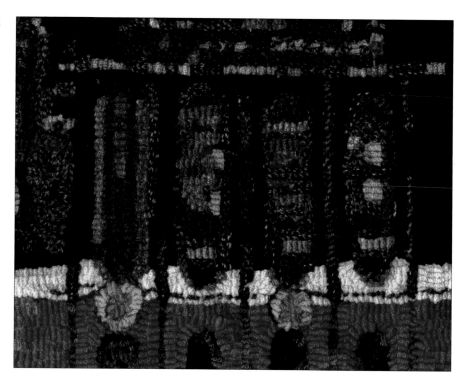

you are looking through one set of windows and out the other side. You see some of the brick from the house in behind, but some of the shadows are from the people on the streetcar.

It was difficult to keep the green-gold of the tree that is just bursting into leaf distinct from the sign with Chinese characters behind. I had to simplify the decorative pattern of the shingles in the gable of the house.

I did some dyeing for this rug. I overdyed a grey-and-white houndstooth check for the roof shingles with a blue-green. For the

grid-like vent on the roof of the streetcar, I overdyed a piece of black-and-white houndstooth check with Cushing's Aqualon Pink. I also dyed for the light street car parts; they are a mixture of Cushing's Aqualon Pink and Aqualon Blue, spot dyed.

I used Noro woolen yarn for the streetcar and hydro wires, making them shade from black to gray. I had an unusual piece of rusty red dyed over mauve that was perfect for the side of the neighboring house.

I always dip dye my skies. I cut the wool and hook it in the order in which the strips were cut.

Trish Johnson
Toronto, Ontario, Canada

I first saw a hooked rug in 1972. My Aunt Eliza was hooking a rug of a sailing ship and I filled in a lot of the sky for her. From 1990 to 1992, I hooked my first rug. It was pink roses on a black background from a kit. Since then I have hooked a series of rugs on the theme of home. I like rugs with a narrative theme. I try to hook something that has meaning for me.

Across from the Art Gallery of Ontario, 17" x 23½", #3-, 4- and 6-cut dyed and as-is wool on linen.
Designed and hooked by Trish Johnson, Toronto, Ontario, Canada, 2015.

All Creatures Great and Small

I started imagining this rug in my head many years ago but never had the time to actually plan it and draw it out. Initially, I envisioned it a little different than it ended up. I first thought that I would put a faded-out map in the background. However, when I started putting things together on paper, it looked too busy. I had to rethink things. So I started looking online for other options, and when I saw the global latitude and longitude lines, I knew that would work.

Now to plan the animals. I knew from the beginning that I wanted the Biblical lion and lamb lying down together. I also knew that I wanted animals from each con-

tinent. I created the animals individually at first, then played with how to position each one. I used a copy machine to experiment with reducing and enlarging the size of each animal until I was satisfied with the overall look. Many of the small animals, reptiles, and birds are out of proportion to the large animals, and the elephant and giraffe are a little small, but this approach allowed me to fit everything on the rug and to make the smaller animals a reasonable size.

When hooking the animals I used mostly #3- or 4-cut strips in a mix of new and reused wools. The polar bear has 13 different colors in it. I used a lot of tweed and plaids

in many of the animals to give them texture. It was amazing to me that some parts just fell together and others had to be redone several times. For instance, the face of the lion was so easy, but the body I struggled with.

The background also needed attention. It needed to have a global appearance. In order to suggest roundness, I made the top and edges darker and lightened the center. I wanted the longitudinal and latitudinal lines to fade into the background, so I used a #8 cut for them in a light color; that made them visible but not bold. When hooking the rest of the background, I followed the latitudinal lines.

All Creatures Great and Small, 40" round, #3-, 5-, and 8-cut recycled, plaid, and hand-dyed wool on monk's cloth.
Designed and hooked by Ellen Forstrom, North Haledon, New Jersey, 2015.

Ellen Forstrom
North Haledon, New Jersey

I became interested in hooked rugs during a trip to Nova Scotia, where my sister and I found a piece made in Chéticamp. When I got home, I started looking into this art form and found a rug hooking camp nearby. A friend and I went to the camp, and after that I was hooked.

Love the theme of world globe combined with animals; skillful shading of the foliage. Excellent use of color to show longitude, latitude; animals wonderfully hooked, and placement works so well.

Belgians and Berners

This rug was designed from a photograph taken at The Rocks Estate in Bethlehem, New Hampshire. For the past eight years, my husband, Bill Wilczek, and I have taken our dogs there between Thanksgiving and Christmas to raise awareness for "Trees For Troops," which is a national program run by the Christmas Spirit Foundation.

In 2015, the dogs raised $2,500 while greeting visitors, enjoying the attention they received, and having their pictures taken. It is a great way to share our Bernese Mountain Dogs with the community, enjoy the Christmas season at a beautiful tree farm, and raise awareness of this important program that provides free Christmas trees to the families of our military troops.

We currently have four Bernese Mountain Dogs, ranging in age from 8 years to 20 months and covering three generations. When not hooking them, I enjoy working with the dogs for occasional breeding, draft work, conformation, obedience, and therapy dog work. Both my husband and I share our passion for this breed through Wilczek Woodworks, his business of making carts and wagons for dogs. The dogs were originally Swiss farm dogs that were famous for pulling milk wagons from the farms to market. We are often seen at northern New Hampshire and Vermont farmers' markets with the dogs pulling carts and wagons, carrying our purchases back to the car, and giving rides to children.

I feel honored that a previous rug, *Tennescott Four Dog Rug– Bernese Mountain Dogs*, was recognized in *Celebration XXIV*. Both of these rugs were also featured in Judy Carter's book *Hooking Animals: How to Bring Animals to Life in Wool Rugs*. An earlier dog rug was also included in Elizabeth Black's book, *Hooked on the Wild Side*. A two-part article on hooking dog faces also appeared in the ATHA magazine.

I began this rug in 2013 in a class given by Judy Carter at the Hunterdon County Rug Artisan Guild Summer Camp in New Jersey. Judy taught me how to use textured as-is wool, such as plaids and herringbones, to create animal fur and the distinctive look of the background in this rug. It took me a while to enjoy using wool that was not as tightly woven as the dyed wool that I had used in previous rugs. I continued on the rug myself, with help from friends, and in other classes given by Liz Merino, Anne-Marie Littenberg, and Michele Micarelli. It took me a little over two years to complete this project.

In The Judges' Eyes

Exquisite hooking creates powerfully intimate and moving moment; such realistic shading; amazed at the detail, especially in tree behind dogs. Love how sky and ground relate; enjoy the conversation between horse and dog—exchange of glances puts a smile on my face. All textures enhance; snow done so well.

Barbie Beck-Wilczek
Littleton, New Hampshire

I began rug hooking in 2002 in a county adult education course given by Gail Dufresne. I enjoy hooking my beloved Bernese Mountain Dogs, and I had the privilege to first learn about hooking animals in a class given by Elizabeth Black.

Belgians and Berners, 41" x 25", #4-cut as-is textured and a very small amount of hand-dyed wool.
Designed and hooked by Barbie Beck-Wilczek, Littleton, New Hampshire, 2015.

Château de Chenonceau

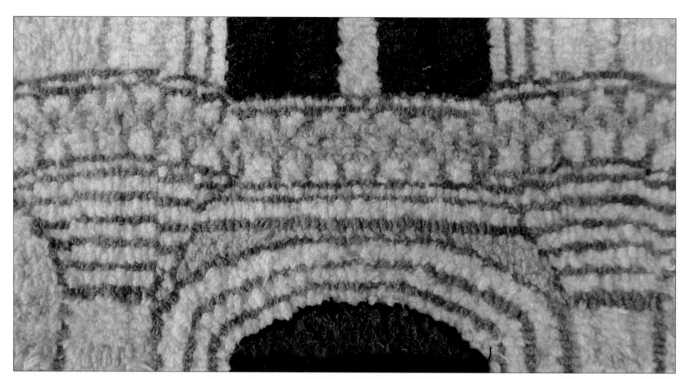

I n 2011, I visited France for the first time. I saw many beautiful things there. I went on an eight-day tour, and we visited Paris, Loire, Mont Saint-Michel, and other famous and picturesque places. I liked France very much.

I have been painting pictures, using the black ink called *sumi*, since 1985. This style of monochrome ink painting is commonly known as Chinese brush painting, but in Japan it is called *suiboku*. I am a rug hooker and also a suiboku painter, as well as a member of one of the boards of the Contemporary Suiboku Painting Association.

I learned rug hooking when I lived in Canada years ago, and that is what made me decide to begin painting pictures after returning to Japan. I learned painting and Japanese calligraphy to make better hooked rugs.

I painted Mont Saint-Michel and created a rug by using the picture as the pattern. Mont Saint-Michel appeared in *Celebration XXV* as an Honorable Mention. Likewise, I painted Château de Chenonceau and made this rug. It is an honor that *Château* was chosen for *Celebration 26*. It took me about a year to complete the rug.

I drew the pattern on rug warp. Then I used Dorr wool, mostly gray graduating to black, and cut it with a #3 cutter. I pulled some old gray and black pieces of clothing from my treasure bag for the ground.

While hooking, I counted the threads of the rug warp to make the château stand straight; I also counted threads between the windows and bricks on the wall. I hooked the château from the foreground to the background. Then I hooked the ground using the clothing in #3 and #4 cuts. The sky was the last part I hooked, and it was boring to hook only white after the complex hooking in the other parts of the rug.

At last it was completed! I am always very happy when I finish a new work.

Fumiyo Hachisuka
Nerima-Ku, Tokyo, Japan

I lived in Toronto, Canada, from 1976 to 1983. I had learned rug hooking under my teacher, Mrs. Fannie Sinclair, from 1979 to 1983. I started teaching rug hooking in Tokyo in 1985, producing an almost-annual exhibition. The 26th Rug Hooking Exhibition will be shown in Gallery K of the Daiichi Hotel, Kichijoji, Tokyo, September 29-October 4, 2016. You can find information at: http://sky.geocities.jp/rughooking234

In The Judges' Eyes

Detail in the decorative stone work and architectural details is amazing; strong contrasts handled deftly. Château itself done with great care; surfaces add excitement to the piece.

Château de Chenonceau, *64" x 52", #3-cut as-is Dorr wool and recycled clothing on rug warp. Designed and hooked by Fumiyo Hachisuka, Nerima-Ku, Tokyo, Japan, 2014.*

Cinque Terre Perspective

I n every aspect of rug hooking there is such diversity. Taking classes provides great opportunities for learning. I eagerly signed up for a class with Pam Bartlett called "Wind and Waves," as I had never hooked water or rocks before.

While on a trip to Italy, I took a lot of photos incorporating a wide range of images of water and rocks. I based my design on one of my photos that added another element—the perspective of looking down from above. I find that hooking something personal

makes for greater enjoyment while working on it, and it also makes the finished mat more meaningful.

My color plan was based on my original photo. I dyed all new wool, using a multitude of dyeing techniques such as straight, spot, mottled, wandering, and abrashing.

My biggest challenge was in hooking the rocks. I needed to get the values just right in order to get the dimensional aspect. Getting the separation between the rocks and shadows also required some tweaking.

Sometimes I used a broken line of hooking to achieve this. Crashing waves, the depth of the water, and distance were achieved by dyeing shades of dark and light blue, teal, and turquoise. I used directional hooking extensively throughout.

I chose not to add a border to this piece. For the finishing, I folded the linen to the back and hand-sewed the tape right up to the last row of hooking, then I sewed the tape to the backing.

Val R. Flannigan
Kelowna, British Columbia, Canada

I have been hooking for 16 years. As a lifelong learner, I take classes whenever possible. I have my McGown and Western Canadian teaching accreditation. I am a member of TIGHR, ATHA, Green Mountain Guild, and Prairie Harvest Rug Hooking School. Cinque Terre is my third mat in Celebration.

In The Judges' Eyes

Nice interpretation; beautiful view, well executed; colors work so well creating illusion of depth. Warm stones close by and water far below, well done!

Cinque Terre Perspective, 9" x 17", #4-cut wool on linen.
Designed and hooked by Val R. Flannigan, Kelowna, British Columbia, Canada, 2014. GRAEME FLANNIGAN

Cobble Bridge

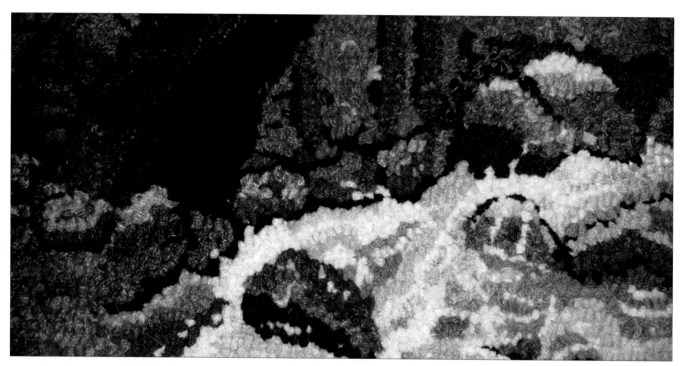

I first became aware of the beauty and range of possibilities that rug hooking offered at a hooking exhibit sponsored by the Hook and I (our local hooking group) founded by a friend, Patti Wharton. After seeing Patti's collected work at her memorial party, I decided to try my hand at the craft. In years past I had braided rugs, and I found I missed the tactile pleasure of working with wool. I ordered some basic supplies from Dorr Mill and jumped in!

I feel fortunate to live minutes away from Acadia National Park, which offers endless inspiration and challenge. One of my favorite locations is the Cobble Bridge, one of 17 granite bridges built by John D. Rockefeller, Jr., as part of a 44-mile network of carriage roads. The Cobble Bridge was the first bridge, completed in 1917, and the only one constructed from beach cobbles rather than cut granite.

Capturing this much-loved spot in wool was a real joy. I admit that doing the moving water was daunting. I sat on the bank studying the water, trying to "pixelate" the movement and the colors of "wet" in my mind.

I used purchased hand-dyed wool—some with a shimmery backing, which gives the water some sparkle. I do not draw well, so I always start with the horizon lines. For static features, such as the bridge, I take photos, enlarge them on a copier to the appropriate size, and trace their outline on the foundation cloth. Then I fill in with what I see. I'm never afraid to tear out areas that don't work well; I will redo an area until it does work before finally declaring victory.

To date I have completed 14 rugs, all but one of them Acadia landscapes. My very supportive husband had cards printed with images of my work titled "Visions of Acadia."

I enjoy seeing peoples' reactions when they recognize the places depicted in my rugs. Whether blue skies or storm clouds, mountains topped with fog or snow, or the tender colors of spring, Acadia National Park is constantly changing. I could spend several lifetimes trying to capture its essence. Eventually I want to expand my subject matter, but for now I'm completely happy with my Acadian landscapes.

Mary D. Hays
Bass Harbor, Maine

Mary started hooking in 2011, learning through books, YouTube videos, and the constructive criticism of friends and experienced hookers. She has won several "best in show" awards at Maine events. Cobble Bridge is her first rug to be featured in Celebration.

In The Judges' Eyes

Perfectly executed cobblestones, water, and rocks; values and colors spot-on. Each tree is unique, stone colors make the bridge stand out, but the most exciting part is the rushing water.

Cobble Bridge, 38" x 25". #3- to 4-cut hand-dyed wool on rug warp. Designed and hooked by Mary D. Hays. Bass Harbor, Maine, 2015.

Giraffes

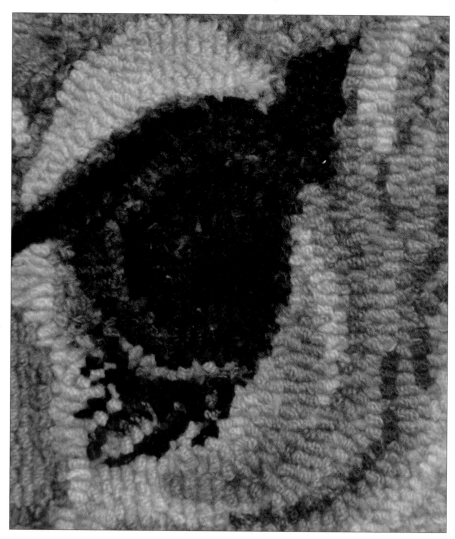

Two passions, rug hooking and traveling, fill my time. I have traveled the globe to fulfill my travel passion, and crossed the U.S. numerous times to avail myself of the guidance of my mentor, Diane Stoffel.

I like to memorialize my trips by bringing home unique pieces of fine art, fiber art, and musical instruments. I also like to reinterpret some of my trips into fiber art projects. Such is the case with *Giraffes*. The inspiration for this piece came from a safari in Kenya. Fascinated with the elegance and structure of the several species of giraffes, I chose to commemorate this trip by hooking a piece featuring these long-necked wonders. After reviewing hundreds of photos from the safari, I decided on a collage approach.

Enlarging the details of the giraffes allowed me to utilize my preferred fine cuts for detail and shading. The intricate, delicate, subtle shadings of the animals in their foliage habitat presented both a challenge and a learning experience.

The majority of the wool was new, overdyed wool, most of which was taken from my large personal stash. In each of my pieces I include wool left to me by my late aunt, Jan Leavitt, who introduced me to rug hooking. The as-is green plaid fabric used in the borders was from Jan's stash. By using Jan's wool, I honor the memory of the person who lit the fire of my passion for fiber art.

Hooking this piece was both a labor of love and an attempt to create a piece of art that would evoke the intimate perspective and unique feelings from my Africa trip. It hangs in the entry of my home, not far from *African Sunset*, which was previously featured in *Celebration XIX*.

Other works of mine that have appeared in *Celebration* include *Crown Prince* (*Celebration XIV*); and *Waging Peace, Fighting Disease, Building Hope* (*Celebration XXI*.)

In addition, my work has been honored with many first place, division, and best-of-show awards at the Orange County Fair. The Los Angeles County Fair has awarded many first-place ribbons, as well as several special judges' awards to my work. *Giraffes* earned first place and was named best of show at the 2015 Los Angeles County Fair.

Susan Naples
Santa Ana, California

Susan began rug hooking over 20 years ago, working under the guidance and tutelage of acclaimed rug hooking teacher Diane Stoffel for 15 of those years. She has completed about 30 hooked pieces. Giraffes is her fourth rug to be included in Celebration.

In The Judges' Eyes

Superb color choices for spots; interesting, creative animal study. Good color gradations with visually graphic subject matter.

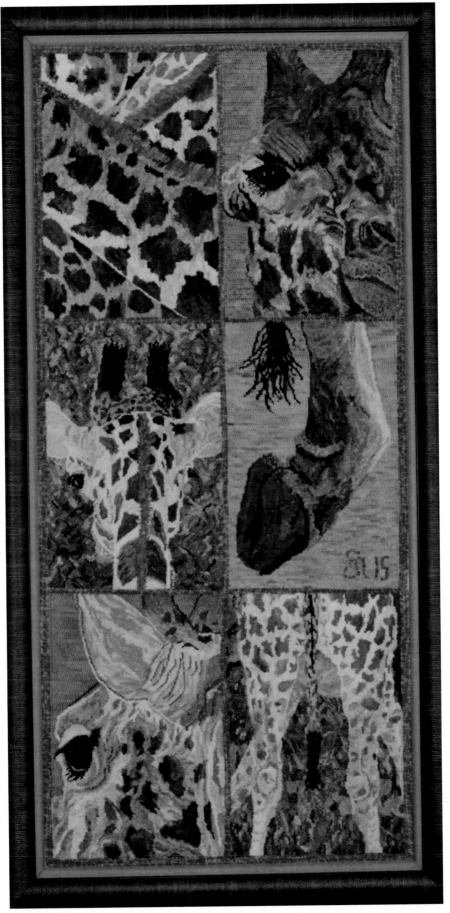

Giraffes, 22" x 47", #3-, 4-, and 5-cut overdyed wool on rug warp.
Designed and hooked by Susan Naples, Santa Ana, California, 2015.

Hi Daddy, I'm Sophie

My husband was diagnosed with Lewy Body Dementia (much like Alzheimer's) on April 30, 2014. Two days later I took a photo of him—sitting in his favorite chair, talking with his buddy, Sophie. The photo turned out so well that I knew I had to hook it.

Three areas are the focus: Del, Sophie, and the background. Color planning was easy, because I simply used the colors that were in the photo.

I started with Del's shirt. It is a brown, blue, and gray plaid, and it looked like it would be difficult to hook. I drew it on the backing and just hooked one color at a time. It was so simple and fun; I loved it.

I felt that the main focus of the rug should be my husband's face, so I concentrated on that. Dyeing the wool was fun! I used many techniques with many recipes, trying to get just the right values. Using a very small cut of wool allows me to blend the colors. I looked repeatedly at my husband's face in different lights in order to choose the correct colors, and after many, many hook-and-rip attempts, I am happy with the way it looks. His nose was the most difficult because he has a one-of-a-kind nose; besides it is a profile, so it had to be perfect. Our whole family loves the rug and says it looks exactly like my husband.

For Sophie: Her long hair is silver and white, very soft and fluffy, so I simply added color where it was on the photo. The hair was a little difficult to hook in tiny, single strands because of the fluffiness.

I got the idea for the background of this rug when a friend looked at the original photo and saw that I had one of my hand-made quilts on the wall behind Del. She asked me if I was going to use that in the rug. I thought about it for a long time.

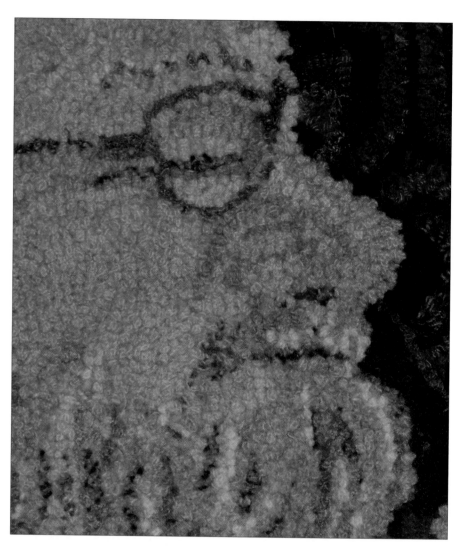

I decided the hexagons would look good, but that I should hook the background in several colors that would complement my husband's shirt and the rest of the rug. To enhance the light color of the dog, I chose a dark background. When color planning my rugs, I find that I use the colors from my reference photos. The only colors I added are in the background, and I tried to use complementary colors there. I'm happy with it.

The rug will hold great memories of Del and his little buddy, Sophie.

Marilyn D. Becker
Wausau, Wisconsin

Being interested in genealogy led me to my love of hooking portraits. I've been hooking rugs for three years, and I can't wait to start the next one. "Hi Daddy, I'm Sophie" is my third rug accepted for Celebration.

"Hi Daddy, I'm Sophie", 36" x 26", #3- and 4-cut hand-dyed, as-is, and repurposed wool on rug warp. Designed and hooked by Marilyn D. Becker, Wausau, Wisconsin, 2015.

Jasper

I began this project as a gift for my mother. Jasper was a Bullmastiff and my mother's service dog. He was her constant companion, helped her with anxietyin public, and was able to help Mom get back up if she had fallen.

I created the flag background to honor my mother's involvement with the VFW and her husband's military service.

This pillow is only my third hooked piece. It took me about a year to complete due to difficulties with hooking the eyes and muzzle. I had started with the eyes and shading around them, but something didn't look right, and I couldn't move past them. No matter how much I looked at them, I just couldn't find the problem. It wasn't until I began looking at other Bullmastiffs at a dog show that I realized that the color of my

dog's eyes were too light. I reverse-hooked just the iris of each eye, and the problem was completely fixed. I was able to move on from there.

My next challenge was getting the depth and detail of his "black" muzzle. I wanted to show the detail of the wrinkles and even whisker bumps that make up the muzzle. The transitional shading, between the muzzle and his face, includes darker browns and tans that give depth and dimension. When I showed the finished pillow to our own dog, he barked at it, unsure if it was another dog or not. I guess I got the eyes and muzzle right.

The blacks and various grays of the piece are from recycled wool. The beiges, browns, and tans are both dyed and Dorr gradient bundles. These give all of those nice bright-

to-dark hues that are everywhere on the dog's body.

It was important to me that the piece did not turn out to be just a tan dog. I paid special attention to the placement of loops in order to give the hair direction and to create more definition of the body shapes.

For the flag background, I used overdyed white plaid for the red and blue, and a white skirt for the white. For finishing the pillow, I found a skein of yarn that had many of the colors from both the hooked part and the star backing. This yarn brought everything together nicely. The edges are whipped, and I liked the tassels as an added touch.

Sadly, Jasper passed away just a few months after I completed this pillow. Mom now keeps this pillow as a reminder of him.

Judy L. Billen
Stanfordville, New York

I enjoy many crafts, including jewelry making, creating rustic furniture, and straw bale gardening. I was introduced to rug hooking about three years ago by a friend. My favorite subjects are animals.

In The Judges' Eyes

Snout looks almost three-dimensional. Terrific, clever background enhances this portrait; particularly nice finishing job.

Jasper, 14½" x 11", #3- to 4-cut as-is and hand-dyed wool on monk's cloth.
Designed and hooked by Judy L. Billen, Stanfordville, New York, 2015. ON LOCATION STUDIOS, INC.

Life Is a Beautiful Ride

We are lucky to have so many beautiful rug hooking designs available for purchase. Even so, I have discovered that I get the most joy and sense of accomplishment when finishing something that I created from beginning to end. The path to my designs is often winding, with many twists and turns. I begin with one idea and usually end up with something very different when I am done.

This rug is a good example of that crazy process. The inspiration for this design began with a simple vintage Japanese matchbook cover illustrating men riding a bicycle built for five. It looked fun and whimsical! However, something happened during the sketching phase, as it often does, and the result is what you see.

I admire all different styles of rugs, but mine are usually made with #4, #6 and #8 cuts because those are the cutters I have in my collection. Occasionally I hand cut one of those strips in half if something smaller is needed. Most of the wool in this rug is off-the-bolt and recycled pieces. The letters and sky were hand dyed. The biggest challenge for me with this rug was the streamers on the bike. I wanted them to stand out a little to give the rug dimension. I lost track of how many different fibers and fabrics that I hooked in and pulled out to get the texture I was seeking. Sari silk finally gave the streamers movement and a shimmer that I was looking for.

I am known as a slow, high hooker to my friends in the rug hooking world. As a resident of Colorado, this description of my style inspires a lot of creative comments! I enjoy hooking with other people and participate in several different rug hooking groups, including Colorado ATHA. We have a wonderful, eclectic array of rug-hooking styles represented in our group, and I am constantly in awe of the talent and creativity. *Life Is a Beautiful Ride* is my second rug selected to appear in *Celebration*.

Shawn Niemeyer
Centennial, Colorado

I have had my hands in some type of art or craft since I can remember. My interest in rug hooking materialized and grew for many years before I found an instructor and picked up a hook. I pulled my first loop in the fall of 2008, and now I cannot imagine life without rug hooking!

Life Is a Beautiful Ride, 31" x 26", #3- to #8-cut as-is and hand-dyed wool and sari silk on monk's cloth. Designed and hooked by Shawn Niemeyer, Centennial, Colorado, 2015.

Irregular border is perfect choice for this whimsical piece; great technical skills; a little gem. Wonderfully creative border and superb finishing technique around each scallop. A positively buoyant rug.

Lisa Dancing

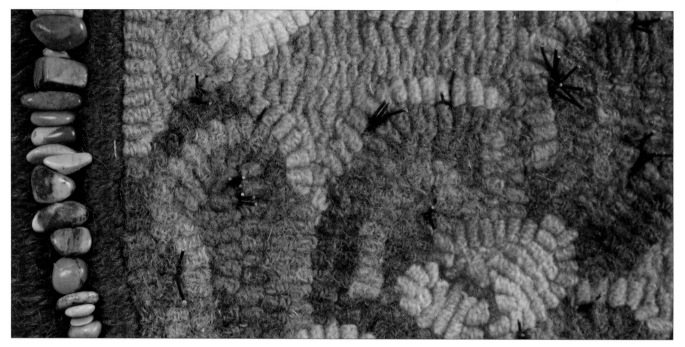

The inspiration for this rug is my sister, Lisa Sue Hill. I have watched her for 15 years as she has dealt with the onset of several autoimmune diseases. After many years of medical tests, special diets, medications, and surgeries, she finally received the diagnosis of lupus, fibromyalgia, and rheumatoid arthritis. It has been her faith in God and passion for her calling in life that give her the strength to keep going and make her my hero.

Lisa teaches special needs children in the sixth, seventh, and eighth grades. She loves the challenges of discovering how each individual student learns, then creating ways to teach each student so they can comprehend. It is her calling and her passion.

She is the mother of two busy teenagers and is devoted to her family.

There is much symbolism in the rug. Lisa was a ballerina in her younger life and still carries that grace with her, so I depicted her in a ballerina leap. The desert, cactus, rocks, and weeds represent the hard, painful, and lonely places that people with autoimmune diseases often face. They are misunderstood because they look just fine on the outside but are anything but fine on the inside. They have good days, bad days, and absolutely awful days, and it is completely unpredictable. People often think they are using their disease as an excuse, because one day they may need to be in bed but the next they seem just fine. It is hard to understand until someone close to you has one of these diseases.

I used copper jewelry wire for the cactus needles and stones in the binding because I wanted to emphasize the painful parts of having autoimmune diseases.

The two ribbons symbolize Lisa's two children, whom she teaches to be strong through her own example of determination, and her dependence on her faith to sustain her.

The three birds symbolize her faith. She trusts in God, and He's always there to lift her up and encourage her in the quiet and unfailing way that God works in each person's life.

I used spot dyes, overdyes and as-is wool. I dyed swatches for Lisa's skin. Her face details were hooked with embroidery floss. I used #3 through #6 cuts. The rug is mounted on wood paneling, covered front and back with acid-free foam board.

Melody Hill Lavy
Woodway, Texas

I now live in Waco, Texas, and have a wonderful group of friends to hook with. I was taught by Susan Quicksall in 2003. I love to design patterns and dye wool. I am currently attending the McGown Teachers Workshop.

In The Judges' Eyes

Appreciate the realism of the human form in this piece; unique and creative finish. Soft colors give a gentleness; expressive and uplifting. Gorgeous cacti; wonderful movement of the dancer.

Lisa Dancing, 18" x 31", #4-, 5- and 6-cut wool, embroidery floss, jewelers' wire, and turquoise stones on linen.
Designed and hooked by Melody Hill Lavy, Woodway, Texas, 2015. JOE GRIFFIN

mirrormirror

I have discovered that my hooking projects always seem to find me—not the other way around! I may have an idea of what I want to hook, and I may even spend time thinking about it. Then one day, a picture will drop from a photo album and all my thinking changes.

That is what happened with *mirrormirror*. I was in the middle of my last rug when a photo of fall foliage reflected in a pond literally dropped into my lap. I was reminded of how much I loved the absolutely still, reflective water in this picture and the graphic nature of its center pattern. I knew immediately that this was my next rug, and I couldn't wait to get started.

The where and when of this image are hazy. I was driving through the Adirondacks when I saw this amazing end-of-day scene. I stopped the car to take a photo. I am very glad I did.

Initially, I was concerned about the excessive detail of the picture. To develop this design, I drew it three times. With each drawing, detail naturally fell away and I began to think this rug might be possible . . . but a struggle to tame.

How much detail is enough to give reality to the trees? How much detail is too much and detracts from the pattern and color that drew me to the photo in the first place? Each step of the preparation process made the image more abstract. I had not started out wanting to hook an abstract image, but I thought that might be where I was heading.

Nancy Thun
Hoboken, New Jersey

I found my way into rug hooking in 2009 when I saw someone hooking with yarn. Now I could spend my entire day hooking and binge-watching TV. A set designer, I work on Broadway with London-based designers.

In The Judges' Eyes

Darker values in the mirror image of the lake provide tremendous realism; wonderfulwonderful! Gorgeous study; peaceful and serene. Amazing! Great handling of color and form.

Once I started hooking, I was over-whelmed by the mirror aspect of the piece. However, I knew from my drawing that the mirroring was not exact; there were differences between the halves. I decided to focus only on what was on my frame and hook what I saw, just the pattern and color.

I was surprised when I first laid out the rug and saw how close the halves were, how much the bottom reflected the top. After that I let go and hooked. The piece itself decided how pictorial it would be.

When finished, I felt a rush of relief and release—and melancholy. This is a big, complex rug. I was happy and I felt very tired.

Then another picture "fell" out of the photo album . . .!

mirrormirror, 68" x 26", hand-dyed 3-ply bulky wool yarn on rug warp. Designed and hooked by Nancy Thun, Hoboken, New Jersey, 2015.

Mother Goose

I've been creating hooked rugs for years, and I love doing it. I have more ideas for new rugs than I have time to hook them, but sometimes I get an idea that stays with me and demands that I see it through. The *Mother Goose* rug was just such an idea.

I drew the goose design years ago—a simple white goose in a pasture with familiar Mother Goose elements at her feet: a black sheep, a pumpkin, Humpty Dumpty, and Mary, Mary, Quite Contrary. The cow was jumping over the moon behind her in the composition. But it was very plain, the elements were dull, and I only hooked the goose's head before abandoning the whole thing.

Fast-forward to the present, when I decided I still wanted a *Mother Goose* rug, so I pulled out the old design and started to evaluate where it went wrong. It occurred to me that the setting was a problem.

In the interim, I had been working with Victorian themes in my steampunk rugs, so I moved my goose into a different setting: a Victorian library. I converted her into a goose person so she would fit nicely within that setting. She wears a purple satin gown, is sitting in front of a large window, and at her feet are her imagined nursery rhyme children.

From the original design I kept the cow jumping over the moon, as well as Humpty Dumpty and Mary, Mary, Quite Contrary. The pumpkin was upgraded to include Peter and his wife, and I added the One, Two, Buckle My Shoe boy and Ride a Cock Horse to Banbury Cross.

I chose a limited color palette to keep the rug unified and balanced. The colors are greens, oranges, purples and blues, with cream as a neutral. The challenge was to create a variety of values and tones that tie the whole image together without running the same colors into each other in the composition. The orange, for example, is displayed in bright values for her beak and in the pumpkin, but dulled down for clothing and the window frame. This allows continuity in the rug without using a full spectrum of colors.

I started hooking the rug at the end of February 2015 and completed it in May 2015. I enjoyed hooking it, I felt like I successfully captured the image I truly wanted, and I love it!

Donna K. Hrkman
Dayton, Ohio

Donna has been an artist all her life. Rug hooking allows her to express her creativity and love for design. She's written two books and teaches across the country. She loves sharing her work. This is her ninth Celebration finalist.

Mother Goose, 36" x 46", #3-cut hand-dyed wool on linen.
Designed and hooked by Donna K. Hrkman, Dayton, Ohio, 2015.

My Feathered Friend

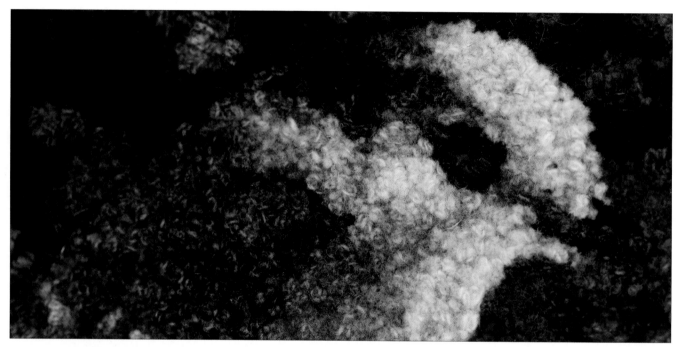

On a winter's day, in Canada's great northern forests, often the call and soft chatter of gray jays can be heard as they silently glide from tree to tree. They are absolutely delightful birds to watch. Occasionally, while walking through the woods, you can catch a glimpse of a jay quietly observing its surroundings.

My *Feathered Friend* shows the gray jay from a quieter side as he graces us with his presence, silent and motionless for a moment, resting on a branch close to the tree trunk. This awe-inspiring moment provided a closer look at the gray jay and the opportunity to observe the purity and beauty of our feathered friends.

My composition commenced with an in-depth study of my subject. I expressed nature's many beautiful colors through the use of hand-dyed woolen fabric in a variety of textures and plaids related to what I see. Designed on linen, along with an extensive color palette, each fine cut, hooked visually, brings my subject more alive.

Art gives people the opportunity to challenge themselves—if they will accept the challenge. The gray jay challenged me to go beneath the surface of the lines—to redefine them with precise colors and shading that would re-create his incredibly thick plumage and details. This challenge unveiled *My Feathered Friend*.

Art is viewed by many; however, once in a while a new viewer shows up to critique your work. Witnessing a new viewer's reaction to a finished piece is always rewarding.

When my piece was completed, it was time to display it in our living room. Unexpectedly, our puppy became very interested in my piece. She sat and stared at the bird for some time, expecting it to fly out of the frame at any moment. Her emotional response was a new keynote for me in terms of experiencing art being viewed by others.

In The Judges' Eyes

Love the sharp detail of the bird against slightly blurry background of the tree; masterful blending of colors to obtain muted effect. Amazing! Looks like a photograph.

Diane Ayles
Huntsville, Ontario, Canada

"Expressing my love of nature with this medium is a beautiful journey," says Diane Ayles, an international award-winning artist. Diane has been recognized for her contributions to the advancement of rug hooking by the Hooked Rug Museum of North America and was named Canadian Artist of the Year in 2015. Her work was featured at the Ontario Hooking Craft Guild 50th Annual Hooked Rug Show. My Feathered Friend is her third piece to be featured in Celebration.

My Feathered Friend, 17½" x 12", #2- and 3-cut hand-dyed wool on linen.
Designed and hooked by Diane Ayles, Huntsville, Ontario, Canada, 2014. TYLER AYLES PHOTOGRAPHY

Offshore Hooking

Every family enjoys sharing an activity that brings them together, and in my family it's fishing. Now that our two sons are grown, it is understandable that a fishing rod would be thought of with high regard. We have been able to fish our favorite places—surf fishing on Hatteras Island and at home on the Chesapeake Bay. The most coveted fishing trips have been, and still are, offshore from Oregon Inlet, North Carolina.

A day out in the Gulf Stream is filled with excitement and adrenaline, whether it's catch-and-releasing white and blue marlin, or catching yellowfin tuna and mahi mahi for dinner. The photo for this rug was taken returning from one of these memorable trips out on the water. It captures the rush of the wind and the dampness of the salt spray.

Once I saw the photo, I knew it had to be a rug! During the early planning stages of this rug, I knew I was onto something. It piqued an interest with the men of my household that no other floral or pictorial ever had.

I knew this would be the perfect project to start with Ingrid Hieronimus in an upcoming workshop at The Maryland Shores Rug Hooking School. I transferred the pattern, and Ingrid dyed the wool, using the photo as a guide.

An 8-value custom swatch, ranging from bright gold to dark brown, was used for the reel. The water was a combination of several different spot dyes, swatches, and solids. An overdyed texture was used as a small border just inside the frame.

The most challenging part was distinguishing the many textures of the metal that made up the reel and reel seat. Some areas were smooth and reflective, with nicks and scrapes, while others had threaded patterns of ridges.

My favorite part was hooking the fishing lure. I especially enjoyed re-creating the movement of the skirt of the lure as it was tossed about by the wind and spray. I was able to give the shiny metal a subtle shimmer by using a gray dip-dyed metallic wool.

Offshore Hooking was professionally framed and will be hung in our second home in Southport, North Carolina.

Pam Manders
Arnold, Maryland

Mary Lou Bleakley, a dear friend of my late mother, taught me how to pull my first loops in 2007. Since then, I have completed 14 rugs. Offshore Hooking is my first rug to be featured in Celebration.

In The Judges' Eyes

Riveting composition hooked with minute details; can almost hear the waves crashing! Gorgeous depth of field; feels like you could reach out and touch this reel. Less is more, and you feel the sea.

Offshore Hooking, 31" x 22", #3- and 4-cut hand-dyed wool on rug warp. Designed and hooked by Pam Manders, Arnold, Maryland, 2015.

On the Outside Looking In

Living in the farming suburbs of Philadelphia, I was imagining how I could bring some of this country charm inside my home. I decided on a chicken rug that I would place in my eat-in kitchen. I measured the area to decide on my finished rug size. I used a roll of wrapping paper, cut to the determined size, as my draft canvas.

Not knowing anything about chickens personally, I quizzed a dear family friend who had worked at a hatchery as a boy. I was concerned that there should be a sense of community in the chicken yard, so I asked Larry, "Are there some types of chickens that don't like other chickens?" To this day, we get a good giggle out of how silly that sounded. To his knowledge, he said, he really didn't think so. That's when I decided my chickens of choice would all be friends.

My go-to place for visual references is Google images. My search made me realize that chickens must be very hard to photograph because they simply don't stay still; so most of the pictures were blurry. I made my final selection of chicken images and copied them into a Word document, resizing them to be consistent. I used a photocopier to enlarge as needed. I printed the final images out in color to help with color planning. Using tracing paper, I outlined my chicken subjects and cut each out individually before playfully placing them where I wanted them in the scene. Once happy with the design, I used a light table to trace it on to my linen backing.

Now that I had my pattern figured out, I took it to a rug camp taught by Jen Lavoie in Cape May. I started hooking the chickens first and found that textured wool worked in my favor. One of Jen's lectures taught me that the background should be hooked straight, in order to appear still, and the subjects should be hooked with directional hooking to show movement.

I was undecided on where to place the black-and-white chicken, so I put her "on the outside looking in." It was then that I realized I had the title to my rug. My biggest challenge was hooking the chickens' feet. The solution was to darken the shadow beneath each chicken to provide more contrast. Jen advised me to use a non-organic color for the border of this very organic scene, and it worked well. After two years in the works, this rug now hangs above my kitchen table, where I can tell guests all the stories of how it came together.

In The Judges' Eyes

Great original composition with fabulous border that adds so much. Appreciate the time it took to hook chicken wire; attention to the wire detail is beautiful. Exceptionally well balanced in design and color. Chicken outside coop a clever concept; different colors in chickens fascinating.

On the Outside Looking In, 44" x 20", #3- to 6-cut textured wools, spot-dyed a background and hand-picked overdyed wool on linen. Designed and hooked by Jennifer O'Malley, Telford, Pennsylvania, 2015. CINDY MACMILLIAN

Jennifer O'Malley
Telford, Pennsylvania

Jennifer holds a Bachelor's degree in Fine Art. She started her journey with rug hooking 17 years ago, experimenting with a kit of recycled wool, then moved on to designing 25 of her own original rugs. Jennifer credits her skills to classes, workshops, camps, and the many rug hooking friends she calls "her people." This is her first appearance in Celebration.

Quiet Dream

It started with a teacup and saucer. Several years ago, our local hospice organization had a tea party for volunteers and—because a second-hand shop supports our hospice programs—all volunteers received a used teacup and saucer. I'd been thinking about hooking and braiding a kimono for several years. Their gentle and graceful designs had captivated me. I even purchased a basted-only kimono at an auction in Maine: the pieces had been cut but never sewn together. The colors of the real kimono and the teacup and saucer seemed to complement each other, and so I had my colors.

My sister and I decided to collaborate on the design elements of the kimono; we picked 10 themes and the same basic traditional shape. My sister, Lynn Hoeft, is a watercolor artist. *Quiet Dream* is looking at the back of the kimono with the arms to the side. It is three dimensional, as there are two gusset-like pieces of hooking to give the look of a real kimono hung on a wall.

The leaves were wet felted and hand stitched to the linen backing before any hooking was done. This piece was hooked in 11 smaller pieces and joined together with braid. I knew I wanted to have a water feature separating the two main joined-together pieces. I thought using a combination of silk, wool, and taffeta would make the water sparkle and shimmer but not compete with the pink and oranges of the rest of the background.

Norma Batastini, Stephanie Krauss, Mary Lee O'Connor, and I dyed the wools. I dyed the silks and fibers for the wet felting; the taffeta is polyester. The shrimp color used in the lanterns and the fan is real kimono silk, embossed with an unusual pattern, as is the back. The river is braided with seven hooked shapes, using the same colors that

are in between the braids. The stems are maroon crushed taffeta. The collar is silk I dyed from a small piece of silk brought to me by my friend Vicki, whose son lives in Tokyo. Most of the silks are charmeuse and crepe de Chine.

It was a challenge to fit everything together and make the pieces the exact same size, but I reminded myself that this is fabric

and braid—and flexible. I am always thinking about how to incorporate braid into a hooked design and hooking into a braided design. One is not more important than the other and they must be complementary. My favorite challenge is going back and forth among my most favorite mediums, which now include wet felting.

Kris McDermet
Dummerston, Vermont

I began braiding and hooking in the late 1970s. I've taught courses in both braiding and hooking in Vermont and making combination rugs in the United States, Australia, and England for the last 30+ years. I'm a member of the Green Mountain Rug Hooking Guild, ATHA, TIGHR, and a local rug hooking/braiding group of 15.

Quiet Dream, 37½" x 43", wool, sari silk, and silk taffeta on linen.
Designed, hooked, wet felted, and braided by Kris McDermet, Dummerston, Vermont, 2015. ALBERT KAREVY

Room with a View: Sea Cave, San Josef Bay, Vancouver Island

In August 2000, my husband and I traveled out to the rugged northwest coast of Vancouver Island and camped on the edge of Cape Scott Park. We hiked in to San Josef Bay, where I discovered a sea cave. Standing inside, mesmerized, I snapped photos of the rock around and above me, the maidenhair ferns like lace around the cave entrance, and the misty scene of sand, ocean, and distant shore.

The impact of this experience stayed with me. I knew there was a rug in it.

I began working on the rug a couple of years later, when someone gave me a black wool coat that I cut into #9 strips and used to hook the black cave surround. Then I stalled. I knew I wanted to depict the scene I had experienced, but, perhaps more importantly, I wanted to convey some of the feeling of that experience! I felt utterly incompetent to complete the remainder of the rug well enough to do either of these things. So the rug start was stored—with the occasional longing look—for over 10 years.

Then along came TIGHR 2015 with its theme of "Back to Nature." This was the push I needed.

I had learned a lot from my hooking in the intervening years, but still this San Josef scene turned out to be the most challenging piece I'd ever done. I cut #4 to #8 strips of as-is new and recycled wools. I hooked, then rehooked. I spent hours dyeing fabrics, attempting to get the exact colors I wanted; colors and fabrics I *knew* would be right

turned out to be totally wrong. But after months of work, I completed the rug in September 2015.

What did I learn from hooking this rug? Well, first, that "gray" isn't just "gray"—it's white-gray to creamy-gray, blue-gray to brown-gray to black-gray, and all the values in between. Second, even the best-planned rug demands some changes. As I hooked along on it, some "sand" needed to become

"water"; a plain black rock needed to be shades of brown and dark blue instead— changes that led to a more satisfying piece in the end.

And perhaps the most important thing I learned is that I can hook a very challenging piece and that it is worth all the time and all the effort I can put into it.

I'm proud of this piece.

I'm proud of myself for hooking it.

Maia Levine
Gabriola Island, British Columbia, Canada

Maia inherited her Gram's rug hooks and has been rug hooking her own designs ever since—close to 20 years. Her work has been featured and sold in gallery shows on Gabriola and Vancouver Islands. She is honored to have this rug in Celebration 26.

In The Judges' Eyes

A lot of drama. Dark foreground— seldom seen—is dynamic and provocative. Exquisite; wonderful sense of space; surface treatment an extra treat!

Room with a View: Sea Cave, San Josef Bay, Vancouver Island, 33" x 24", #4- to 9-cut hand-dyed and as-is new and recycled wools. Designed and hooked by Maia Levine, Gabriola Island, British Columbia, Canada, 2015. CAROLYN DAVEY, ALEX SMITH

Simply Sunflower

Sunflowers are one of my favorite summertime flowers and design motifs. So when I began designing a rug for my Oxford Rug Hooking Teacher Certification class, *Simply Sunflower* rolled off my pencil. It is a partial close-up of a sunflower with vines and leaves. The requirements for the certification rug were to use different loop heights with the Oxford Punch Needles and the Craftsman's Punch Needle, punching with wool, shading, using novelty yarns, and sculpting and clipping. I hand dyed all the rug yarn and wool for *Simply Sunflower* and used novelty yarns for texture. I used three different sizes of Oxford needles and the Craftsman's needle.

The sunflower petals are shaded using the fingering method, with six different shades of yarn that I hand dyed. I started with the darkest color in the middle, working out to the lightest color, and then finished off with a darker orange all along the border of each petal.

The border was started by punching one row of #6-cut dark blue wool fabric with a #8 needle. Then I punched with yarn, starting with the lightest blue of six colors and the #8 Oxford needle, which gives the longest loop. I changed colors and needle size, ending with the darkest blue and the #10 needle—which has a shorter loop. This gave the frame a high/low effect and a light-to-dark effect. I think this element produced good framing around the sunflower with the dark background.

The center has the most texture. I accomplished this by using different-size needles, including the Craftsman's needle, which creates very long loops. I also used

many novelty yarns, wool strips, and silk to create the texture. Some of the loops are clipped to add a shirred effect.

Punching *Simply Sunflower* was a great learning experience, with many hooking elements learned and practiced.

Simply Sunflower will never be a floor rug. It will hang in my new apartment on my freshly painted green wall, to be enjoyed by me and everyone who visits.

E. Ellen Steiger
Ben Lomond, California

Ellen has been interested in fiber arts since she was able to hold a needle as a child. She is the owner of Needles in the Nest studio and shop; she has published a pamphlet on a new version of the Scandinavian Loop Rag Rug, which she teaches. She is a teacher of punch needle rug hooking certified by the Oxford Rug Hooking School, and a member of the Association of Traditional Hooking Artists, Green Mountain Rug Hooking Guild, Wine Country Rug Hookers, and the Peninsula Rug Hookers Guild.

In The Judges' Eyes

Ombre border really gives glowing quality. Excellent spirals, gorgeous flower center. Strong design with wonderful vines; powerful color combination.

Dear Celebration Reader:

Which rugs are your favorites?

The judges have chosen the finalists—now it is up to you to tell us which of these rugs deserve the honor of being named Readers' Choice winners.

Review each of the winning rugs carefully and make your selections. Mark your choices on the attached ballot and be sure to postmark it before December 31, 2016.

OR, go online to vote! Visit our website, *www.rughooking magazine.com* to view all the Celebration 26 rugs and place your vote there.

RHM appreciates the time you take to give us your Readers' Choice vote. Please help us honor the rug hooking artists represented within the pages of **Celebration 26** by voting for your choice of the best of the best.

Sincerely,

Debra Smith

Editor

RUG HOOKING MAGAZINE
P.O. Box 388
Shermans Dale, PA 17090

Subscription Department
PO Box 2263
Williamsport, PA 17703-2263

Subscription Department
PO Box 2263
Williamsport, PA 17703-2263

Simply Sunflower, 2' x 3', hand-dyed wool, wool yarn, and novelty yarns on monk's cloth using #8, 9, and 10 Oxford punch needles. Designed and hooked by E. Ellen Steiger, Ben Lomond, California, 2015. STEVE GOLDEN

Spices of Maseno

Spices of Maseno emerged from a wonderful month spent in Kenya with my daughter Allyson. We traveled there in 2007 on a mission trip to make chalkboards for outdoor classrooms at 15 orphanage schools around Maseno, Kenya. A Saturday trip through the market of a neighboring village, Luanda, provided rich photography of everything from sardines piled high on tarps to these wonderful bags of rich color and aroma. I took the photograph that inspired this rug, and it is one of my favorite pictures from that experience.

In 2013, I was delighted to see Jen Lavoie was a featured teacher at Rugs by the Sea in Cape May, New Jersey. I jumped at the chance to attend this camp, which had been recommended by a very good friend, Patty. This was to be the best gift I could give myself—the chance to learn from Jen, whose rugs I had admired and loved for many years, coupled with a wonderful week away with my very good friend.

This rug became much more a part of me than I anticipated. Just days before we were to leave, Patty had to pull out of the rug camp after receiving a devastating cancer diagnosis. The crushing sadness of her diagnosis, coupled with her absence, challenged the mood of this trip.

Nevertheless, I arrived at camp with a piece of linen, three bins of wool in every spice color imaginable, and no idea how to translate my picture into a rug. There is a fine line between hooking a bag of powdery spice and hooking a blob. Having the gift of Jen as my teacher pulled me through a multitude of challenges. Hooking a plastic bag with a rolled over top was the most daunting task for the first three days. Jen's perseverance—showing me how to use value swatches to create creases and shadows, and

using a #7 cut of wool in the rug foreground, then reducing to a #4 cut in the background to show perspective—provided many "aha" moments.

Jen O'Malley, a mutual friend of Patty's and mine, was also in my class. We hooked, we learned, we laughed, and we opened a bottle of Chardonnay each day at 4, to

honor Patty who got us to Cape May in the first place.

Spices of Maseno will always hold these memories of special people and meaningful life experiences.

Susan Schulz
Penllyn, Pennsylvania

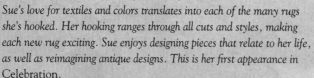
Sue's love for textiles and colors translates into each of the many rugs she's hooked. Her hooking ranges through all cuts and styles, making each new rug exciting. Sue enjoys designing pieces that relate to her life, as well as reimagining antique designs. This is her first appearance in Celebration.

Spices of Maseno, 34" x 24", #3- to 7-cut textured, spot-dyed, and overdyed wool and value swatches on linen. Designed and hooked by Susan Schulz, Penllyn, Pennsylvania, 2015. CINDY MACMILLAN

The Guardian

I'd been thinking of making this rug for years. I'm intrigued by the idea of creating a rug that tells a story and invokes strong emotions. Fairy tales have a very different meaning to us as adults, but we still have strong reactions to them. Fairy tales resonate with each of us according to our own unique childhood memories.

I wanted to make a magical, somewhat eerie design, where Red Riding Hood and the wolf are companions: "You've happened upon them in the woods, and they are looking at you." The mood that I wanted to create is one of serenity, but I'm sure each viewer will feel differently.

Naming this rug was difficult. I didn't want to call it Red Riding Hood or anything so obvious. With Red Riding Hood's hand upon her wolf's head, it's hard to tell who is guarding whom, so I decided to name it *The Guardian*.

I've long admired Michele Micarelli's work and had signed up to take a workshop with her. I wanted to create something special for her class, which gave me the motivation to finally create this rug. Michele dyed the most fabulous wool for this project! I also used beautiful wool dyed by Loretta Scena and Stephanie Allen Krauss.

The wolf is the first realistic animal that I've hooked. Judy Carter's book *Hooking Animals* was very informative. Judy herself gave me a few tips along the way.

This rug started with a drawing. I gathered together the inspirational photos that I'd been saving for years. My daughter Meagan posed for photographs—sitting in different positions with a red chenille blanket draped around her like a cape. When I was unsure of angles, body positioning, or shading, I looked at "how to draw," "art model," and "anatomy" websites, which

were very helpful. My goal was to capture the characters' emotions through facial expressions and body language.

The repetition of making the drawing and transferring it onto linen was a valuable way to familiarize myself with each area of my design.

I often listen to audiobooks while I hook, and I listened to many magical tales while making this rug. I began by first hooking Red Riding Hood's face, then the wolf's. The birch trees had to be hooked next, as they are in the foreground. Hooking the trees was very meditative.

Hooking the red cape was much harder than I had anticipated. My daughter was very patient when asked to model again and again . . .

My biggest challenge was the wolf. There was a lot of frustration and reverse hooking involved, but eventually I was able to understand how to hook fur.

The background was inspired by two gorgeous pieces of wool dyed by Stephanie Allen Krauss. I used about 50 colors from my wool stash to emulate the look of those two pieces of wool. Creating the atmosphere of a misty, magical forest was challenging. One teacher, Loretta Scena, taught me the perfect technique to achieve the results I was looking for.

The Guardian was a great learning experience; it took one year to complete.

Dana Psoinas
Woodbury, New York

Dana has been rug hooking for five years and has made over 20 rugs in various styles. Encouraged by her grandmother, a painter, Dana has been drawing portraits and landscapes for most of her life. Dana loves working with wool and finds great joy in being part of the rug hooking community.

The Guardian, 35" x 47", #3- and 4-cut spot-dyed, dip-dyed, casserole-dyed, dyed swatches and textured wool on linen. Designed and hooked by Dana Psoinas, Woodbury, New York. 2015. EILEEN HARITONIDES

The Tornado in the Pass

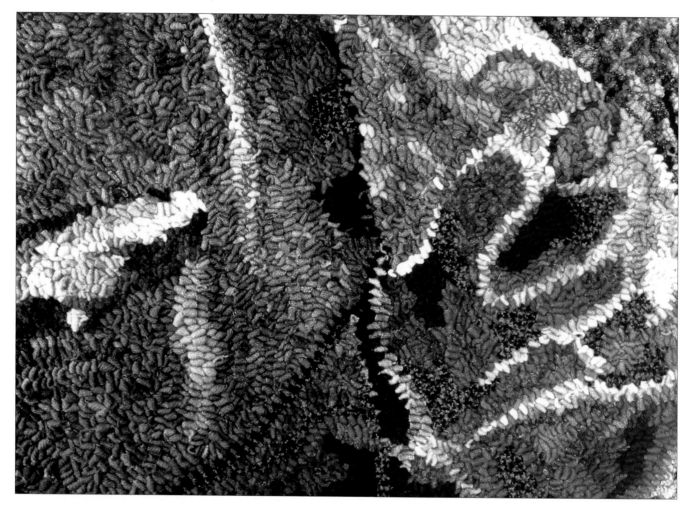

This rug came into existence when our guild had a three-day workshop with Laura Pierce. I chose this picture of my dad taken on a quad (all-terrain vehicle) trip in Tornado Pass, as it captured him in his true element. For the workshop, we were assigned to design a rug with one requirement: The face had to be five inches in diameter. Since I could not bring myself to design the rug without including the cigarette, the rug became larger than life in some ways.

You know you are in for a challenge when the instructor tells you that one of the key elements of the rug—the sunglasses—would be very difficult to hook. But Laura would not let me be defeated, and ignorance truly is bliss; I was able to complete the sunglasses with as-is wool. The face was completed surprisingly easily, considering I was hooking with a #8 cut.

The majority of the rug is as-is wool. The jeans were hooked with wool left over from other projects; I actually used the last inch in the last loop I pulled.

Obviously the shirt is a huge element of the rug. I hand dyed the wool in a seven-value swatch, and the color was perfect. I was not convinced I had dyed enough wool to complete the shirt, but I was sure I could duplicate the color. That belief was tested when I lost a bunch of the wool. My pride took a huge hit when I dyed many yards of wool that came out just too blue. What now?

The shirt was a third of the way done and I was rapidly running out of wool. Then, at a retreat, I found the same color of wool in different values and textures. I took the shirt wool and divided it into three bags: light, medium, and dark. I completed the shirt by pulling random noodles from the bags based on the required shading value.

The border is three hooked rows and two whipped cords, framing the rug and providing stability.

This rug was a challenge from beginning to end, but it did teach me a lot: Yes, you can shade with a #8 cut, and there is a solution to every problem as long as you are willing to think outside the box. I have also learned that each moment of doubt and indecision is worth it in the end, as this forces you to use your creativity. And that gives your rug life.

The Tornado in the Pass, 32" square, #8-cut as-is and dyed wool on monk's cloth.
Designed and hooked by Shelly L. Barber, Okotoks, Alberta, Canada, 2014.

Shelly L. Barber
Okotoks, Alberta, Canada

*My mom had started hooking rugs again and I thought I would try it—
I was hooked. It is just what I was looking for as an artistic outlet. So
11 years and eight rugs later, this is my first submission to Celebration.*

*Nice use of values in clothing and skin
tone. Good cloth rendering; remarkable
color use. Great textures, shadows,
highlights in shirt—well done!*

Through My Eyes (Self Portrait)

While in art school, one of my assignments was to choose a fellow student and create a portrait of him or her—using the least amount of visual information while still capturing a realistic representation and their personality.

I chose to revisit this theme as my concept for this punch-needle rug, using myself as the subject matter. After taking several photographs, I picked one that I thought captured my personality. Using Adobe Photoshop I played with this image, making it a high-contrast black-and-white version of myself, losing all the subtle visual information that wasn't necessary to capture my likeness.

I thought my eyes and glasses told the story best, so I decided to severely crop the photo but keep my hair as an interesting graphic element. I wanted to keep my image for this rug very graphic, using only black and gray wool. Then I decided to add two different pink yarns, suggesting my skin coloring in only a minimal way.

So why the large, colored polka dots? This graphic shape is one that I am very fond of, and I have used them in my illustrations, graphic designs, and as part of my décor in my home. There is nothing I enjoy more than an interesting polka dot shirt! To me the dots capture the fun-loving part of my personality. And the polka dots were the perfect way to add a beautiful color element (three of my favorite colors) to my rug without taking away from my graphic portrait.

The most challenging part of the rug was to complete the assignment that I set up for myself when beginning this project! I am pleased with its outcome, feeling that the end result looks almost photographic from a distance, while still capturing my personality.

I finished Through My Eyes by cording and whip stitching the outer edges; I extended the dots by adding the appropriate colors to this treatment.

This will be my fifth project chosen for Celebration of Hand-Hooked Rugs, and my 16th handmade punch-needle rug completed to date. I prefer using a Craftsman's Punch Needle to hook my designs, using wool rug yarn with monk's cloth as my base. After completing several rugs, I decided that I like short, compact loops best, preferring to use the #9 and #10 settings.

I have several ideas in mind for future hand-hooked projects, which I can't wait to start!

Wayne A. Bressler
New York, New York

Wayne Bressler holds a BFA from Tyler School of Art, Temple University in Philadelphia. He has worked as an art director/graphic designer for various magazine publications in New York City for over 25 years. Wayne enjoys illustrating and cartooning and has had 6 cartoons published in The New Yorker magazine. He continues his pursuit of punch-needle rug making and is always searching for his next inspiration.

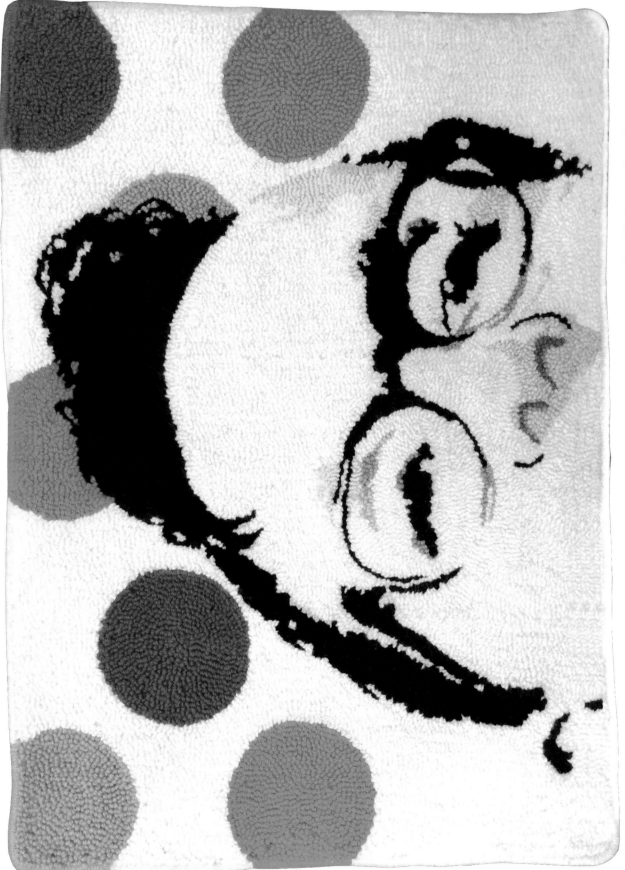

*Through My Eyes (**Self Portrait**)*, 36" x 26", Icelandic Lopi wool yarn and Halcyon Yarn Rug Wool on monk's cloth. Designed and hooked by Wayne A. Bressler, New York, New York, 2015.

Wolfcreek Farm

Hooking *Wolfcreek Farm* was a labor of love. I grew up on this farm with my parents, three sisters, and brother. Though my parents are no longer with us, the farm is still a place we own, love, and cherish.

I had been hooking for less than a year when I received the June/July/August 2014 issue of *Rug Hooking* magazine. I enjoyed the article "Folklife Rugs," by Norma Batastini. Each rug told a very personal story. That same year I was able to see the same story rugs featured in the article on display at Rug Hooking Week at Sauder Village. The seed was planted.

I signed up for my first workshop in October 2014; Cindi Gay was the teacher. I loved her wonderful *Village of Pemberville* rug. The folklife rugs and *Pemberville* inspired me to design our family farm.

At this time, my dear mother was in a hospital. I sat by her bed, sketched, and arranged the buildings, trees, and animals on the drawing with Mother as an active participant. She enjoyed having something creative and hopeful to think about. Over the next three months, she thrilled at seeing each new phase as my hooking progressed.

My parents began farming this property in 1952. It is a traditional Indiana farm that over the years has produced corn, beans, hay, wheat, oats, cows, hogs, chickens, cats,

dogs, and five kids. In designing this piece I eliminated many buildings and much detail in order to tell my story of a simple, charmed, farm life. I enjoyed every aspect of hooking it.

Some of the wool was hand dyed, some off-the-bolt. I did try my hand at dyeing wool for some of the land and used the penny dyeing technique, which Cindi Gay advised, to achieve the shading I needed for the house siding.

The border holds the words G. H. Merson and Family, which was the name we used when showing our Shorthorn cattle in 4-H and open shows.

Starr Atwell
Columbus, Indiana

Starr enjoyed a career teaching art for 28 years. After retiring, a friend invited her to a meeting of a local rug group. She started her first hooked piece that day and now is a member of ATHA and two rug groups in Indiana. Hooking now for three years, she enjoys designing her own rugs which depict animals, people, and life experiences.

In The Judges' Eyes

Very good color choices; nice flow to this story rug. Beautiful details; well-done buildings and good composition; nice handling of lettering.

Wolfcreek Farm, 30" x 45¾", #5- and 7-cut wool on linen.
Designed and hooked by Starr Atwell, Columbus, Indiana, 2015. JOHN RHOADES

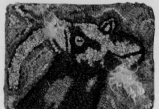

KITS
for all skill levels

BEGINNING · INTERMEDIATE · ADVANCED

We Carry A Wide Range Of *Defranza Designs Kits*

Artichoke

I first saw this pattern at Cedar Lakes Rug Camp and just had to buy it. Most of my rug hooking has been focused on primitive-style wide-cut patterns, but *Artichoke* piqued my interest to hook a smaller-cut rug. Thinking that I would start this rug the following year at Cedar Lakes with the talented Anne Boissinot as my instructor, I asked her to dye the wools I would need. Then, at the very last minute, I couldn't attend camp that year due to a family illness.

I finally started this rug in 2012, under the guidance of June Mikoryak, at a three-day camp hosted by our guild, Buffalo Trace Rug Hookers. I used mainly #4 and #6 cuts for the artichoke itself. This was the smallest-cut rug I had ever hooked, which was

very daunting to me. With June's guidance and her beautiful hand-dyed wools, the body of the artichoke took shape very quickly.

I feel the background in this rug is just as important as the theme. I envisioned using purples and deep blues to highlight the green tones. June suggested using her "hills and valleys" technique to add movement throughout—drawing alternating horizontal and vertical "hills and valleys" lines, then hooking several rows of each. The background is very pleasing to the eye, lively but with dark values. Hooked in #7 cuts, it makes the artichoke itself really pop.

Later that year, I put this rug aside—only about one-quarter done—as the primitive wide cuts were calling for my return! I

brought it back out in 2014 for a few weeks. In the spring of 2015, I decided that I should finally finish *Artichoke* so that I could display it in my newly renovated kitchen.

The original pattern from Roche Riverhouse had a beautiful border, three to four inches wide, of partial artichoke leaves. However, I was running out of wool and ready to finish the piece, so I adapted the pattern by deleting the border, hooking two straight rows of #8 cut, and then simply whipping the edges.

The *Artichoke* rug looks beautiful in my new kitchen. I'm thinking that I will design a companion vegetable pattern to hang with it—possibly a nice bunch of carrots!

Artichoke, 20" x 22¼", #4- to #8-cut hand-dyed wool on linen.
Designed by Roche Riverhouse and hooked by Karen J. Buchheit, Louisville, Kentucky, 2015.

Karen J. Buchheit
Louisville, Kentucky

I'm a former ER nurse but currently focusing on my rug hooking! I started rug hooking in 2009 under the guidance of Jyl Clark. I'm a member of ATHA and Buffalo Trace Rug Hookers, with about 22 rugs completed—a few of my own design.

In The Judges' Eyes

Lovely soft shading and nice energy in the background; exciting use of greens and violets.

Bluegill

I was assigned to teach a class using this pattern at the Northern McGown Teachers Workshop with a one-word directive offered: texture.

Texture can be defined as: 1) the structure, feel, and appearance of something; or 2) a quality that identifies something. In other words, *all* surfaces have visual texture, such as that created by repeating motifs (shape, color, direction, material) in a geometric pattern, or tactile texture, because fibers and objects have physical dimension. Additionally, texture adds contrast without changing colors or value relationships in a composition.

Ultimately, I defined my mission to be an exploration of different ways to build textural effects through the use of both traditional and non-traditional methods and fibers.

I now needed to determine the who, what, where, why and how of a bluegill. I was disappointed to find that the bluegill is actually a drab little fish. However, it does display brighter hues during spawning season, and those are the colors I chose to exploit.

I also found it advantageous to enhance the design by adding elements of the bluegill's natural habitat. This decision facilitated opportunities to include a greater variety of textural effects, as well as providing a visual environment.

I worked this rug with wool from my stash of past and future hooking projects. Since I intended to use the completed piece as a rug, I was limited in the types of alternate fibers I could use. They had to be appropriate for moderate foot traffic, easy to incorporate, and they had to achieve the effect I desired.

Before starting to hook, I reread all my rug-hooking magazines and books to find visual examples of textural techniques that would integrate into an effective whole. Additionally, I found the book *Special Effects Using Creative Stitches*, written by Ingrid Hieronimus and published by her own Ragg Tyme Studio, to be a wonderful resource and guide.

I love the texture of these specialty stitches and learned that they work best when confined to a strict geometric pattern. Therefore, establishing and maintaining the grid for the placement of the loops was of utmost importance. I noted that the grid could be expanded or reduced as necessary to accommodate different widths of fibers, and I found that that purposefully pulling my loops higher—way, way higher than

normal—created the best results.

While hooking *Bluegill*, I prepared the areas to be hand sewn by outlining or filling with "waste yarn." When the fish was completed, I removed the pattern from the frame and used perle cotton or metallic thread and a tapestry needle to affix the shirring to the backing and to secure the "dreads" in their position on the perimeter.

At this point I had one of those "lightbulb" moments. I was inspired to finish the rest of the hooking by working the border and central background entirely off-frame—something completely new and different for me.

Since I am disclosing this here, I guess that decision proved to be successful!

Mary H. Gordon
Street, Maryland

Initially drawn to primitives, Mary began hooking as a creative outlet in 2001. In 2006, she began formal instruction with Peggy Hannum and developed an appreciation of fine shading and dyeing techniques. Mary became a McGown Certified Instructor in 2013 and belongs to the Conestoga and Woolwrights guilds. This is her second appearance in Celebration.

In The Judges' Eyes

Great color choices, especially neutrals, and highly effective use of alternate materials, creative stitches, and applied embellishments. Appreciate the time it took to hook the plaid pattern in the fish.

Bluegill, 22" x 28", #3- hand-cut dyed and as-is-strips; wool and specialty yarns; wool roving, and curlies on linen. Designed by Nancy Jo Finout and hooked by Mary H. Gordon, Street, Maryland, 2015. ROBERT C. GORDON

Chimera

Two months after my return to the United States after nearly 20 years abroad with the military, I took a dye class at Peggy Hannum's house in Lancaster, Pennsylvania. I brought the newly purchased *Chimera* with me. Erika Decree, also attending the class, volunteered to dye the background before her move to Montana. I spent my first open class at Peggy's selecting colors that would give *Chimera* the warm, rich look of an unfaded medieval tapestry.

My first attempt looked nothing like a tapestry, however; even in a #4 cut, my hooked sun looked too crude. Peggy explained that crewel shading would give me the effect I wanted, so I started over. The rug proceeded smoothly though seldom quickly after that, with one big problem: The wool ran out after I had finished the center. Peggy had calculated enough wool to complete the rug according to her technique—and I am a very high hooker.

I decided I should dye at least some of the next batch of wool, though I did ask Peggy to do all the reds and chestnuts for me. I had to redo the first green swatches to copy Peggy's, as mine were too spotty. I also learned that a few grains of complementary color clinging to the haft of the dye spoon will, in fact, make a huge difference in the outcome.

I thought a fringe would work well with *Chimera*. An Oriental fringe, however, seemed too formal; I wanted a more playful and folk-y look. The answer was literally at my feet—I had thrown my almost-finished rug down in my study, on top of my fringed Portuguese Arraiolos rug.

Only one company in Portugal was willing to work with me without a European tax-code number. The sales manager thought it would take 2 to 3 weeks to hand-loom the fringe, as the color—a deep rust that I picked out by number, by its description in Portuguese and in English, and by the colored graphic—wasn't one they normally had in stock.

Two and a half months later, my package arrived from Portugal. Disaster. My fringe was traffic-cone orange. I raced up to Peggy's for formulae to fix the color, which she provided.

I had thought attaching the fringe as I whipped the edge would make the rug stronger. Instead, since the edge of the Arraiolos fringe is by nature uneven, my whipping was lumpy and ragged and slow. I had whipped a quarter of the rug before I gave up and ripped it all out. After whipping the rug in the normal way, I simply attached the fringe with carpet thread, including a fillip at the end. It looks like a sassy tail, but it is really the way the Portuguese include extra wool for repairs.

Barbara Prentice
Springfield, Virginia

Barbara has many artistic members in her family, including professional neon glassblowers, set painters, dollmakers, and quilters; her grandmother was a wool importer. She learned rug hooking while she briefly lived in New England, then spent almost two decades living overseas during her husband's naval career. She now lives in Northern Virginia with her husband and son.

In The Judges' Eyes

Masterful, vibrant, exciting, and happy colors and combinations; many elements work together well.

Chimera, 49½" x 38", #4-cut hand-dyed wool on linen.
Designed by New Earth Designs and hooked by Barbara Prentice, Springfield, Virginia, 2014. IMPACT XPOZURES

Corinthian Prayer

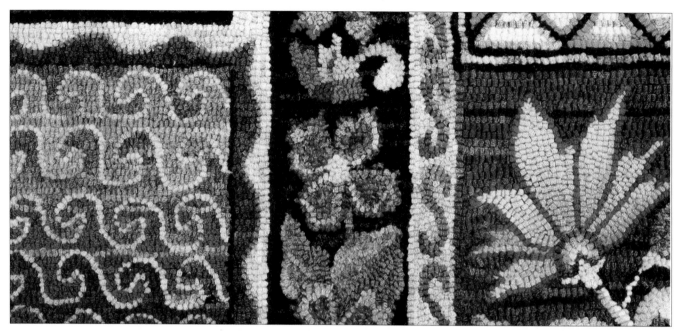

W hat a great opportunity to be assigned to teach *Corinthian Prayer*, by Jane McGown Flynn, at the North Central McGown Teachers Workshop in Newton, Iowa, in April 2015. The *Corinthian Prayer* pattern is an example of a communal prayer rug called a *saph*. This rug is also available in three smaller patterns: *Faith, Hope,* and *Charity*. When I look at this rug, I am reminded that these three things will last forever, and the greatest of these is charity.

One teaching goal was to make this rug look like an ancient Oriental using the colors of the region it would have been produced in. However, I also wanted a rug that would look beautiful in my living room. The way forward was to research and then make compromises where necessary.

My research included finding out what the designer was trying to convey, what type of Oriental pattern this is, what colors are indicated by the origin of the rug design, and how to create the look of a woven Oriental in a hooked rug. Because of the curvilinear design, rounded *mihrabs* (arches), and many flowers, this could be considered a Persian-type design. Pearl McGown suggests, in her pamphlet on hooking Orientals, that when choosing a color plan, we choose one or two dominant colors and then use many values of these colors distributed over the rug to emphasize the motifs that are most important. Persian rugs often included red, old gold, brownish copper, gray-green, navy, and blues. Then the compromising began. Rather than choosing traditional colors, I opted for a more modern color choice of red/orange and blue/green which more closely matches my décor.

In addition to hooking horizontally, rug hookers also use abrashed wool to achieve a woven antique look in Oriental rugs. Four to five different abrashed wools were used in *Corinthian Prayer mihrabs*. The dyeing technique I used to create an abrashed wool with soft edges was to crumple the wool in enough water to allow it to float, layering two to three different dye formulas on top of one another. The fan-like flowers in the *Charity* portion of the rug were dip dyed using one color formula over six colors of wool—natural, pink, green, gray, white, and blue.

The lesson I learned from hooking *Corinthian Prayer* was that while you should know the "rules" for hooking Orientals, it is more satisfying to compromise a little to create a rug that is your own.

A lot of skill—in color choices and technique —to make such a busy design contemplative; lovely use of red and blue gives an authentic Persian rug flavor; beautiful rendition with great care to distribute colors in a balanced way; flowers add excitement.

Darcy Baskin
Benton Harbor, Michigan

Darcy began hooking rugs in 2003. This is her second rug to be published in Celebration. *The first,* Family Memories, *appeared in* Celebration *XX in 2010. She became a McGown Certified Instructor at the North Central McGown Teachers workshop in 2013. Darcy is a member of Lakeshore Rug Hookers in St. Joseph, Michigan, and Strawberry Rug Hookers in Lakeland, Florida.*

Corinthian Prayer, 56" x 36", #3- to 5-cut dyed and as-is wool on monk's cloth.
Designed by Jane McGown Flynn and hooked by Darcy Baskin, Benton Harbor, Michigan, 2015. RHINO MEDIA PRODUCTIONS

Hoot

After hooking shaded flowers—my favorite form of hooking—I suddenly felt a need for something different. Along came *Hoot*. I was taking an online class from Wanda Kerr, and she suggested we look at artist David Galchutt's work. I was hooked! So I decided to ask Connie Bateman, who draws patterns and is a member of our very talented and active ATHA group, to get involved. Off I went to Connie. She got pretty excited about the project, and got in touch with Mr. Galchutt, asking his permission to copy his paintings so I could hook them. Connie was persistent, and he gave in to her charm and gave the go ahead. As a result of these discussions, Connie received the OK to do all his paintings, which she offers through LCs Wool and Silk on Etsy.

Once we had the artist's approval, it was off to the dye pots. Since David's colors were perfect for the piece, I tried to stay with them. I did some swatches, dip dye, and dye by eye. Of course dyeing is the fun part. I used all Woolrich wool, with PRO Chem and Majic Carpet dyes. It's always exciting to see what comes out of the dye pot!

Next, to the hooking: Where would I start? I started with his eyes and nose, and I was off and running. I think my hooking friends thought I was getting senile. This is definitely not the type of thing I would usually hook, but I did get lots of encouragement from them. Of course there's always a problem here or there. The top of the background was cut off in the pattern (as in the painting). I wanted it complete. Luckily Connie left enough fabric on the outside of the design so I could finish the round pattern over his head. I really enjoyed doing his body. There was more shading involved than I thought, especially his wings.

Finally I came to finishing (whipping) around the outer edges. So many colors— how to bring all this together? Recently, at one of our hook-ins, my friend Nancy Parcels had a rug with a double row of whipping. How in heavens name did she do that? Well! I got in touch with Nancy and, true to the generosity of all rug hookers, she sent me the information right away. After doing the first row of whipping, I felt *Hoot* needed three rows. So that is what he has. Last fall, *Hoot* was entered in the Maryland State Fair, where he took First Place and Viewers' Choice awards. So it all worked out great.

Marion Reddy Sachs
York, Pennsylvania
I have been hooking since 1999, after 20 years of making quilts. I studied with Peggy Hannum. My preference is fine-cut (#3) and floral designs. Hoot is my fourth piece to be shown in Celebration, and my first adaptation—of which there will probably be one or two more.

In The Judges' Eyes

Effective mix of hot and cool colors, especially coral "shimmer" around owl; powerful image; good attention to fine detail; reds of leaves complement blues of the bird.

Hoot, 27½" x 42", #3-cut hand-dyed Woolrich wool on monk's cloth.
Designed by David Galchutt and hooked by Marion Reddy Sachs, York, Pennsylvania, 2015. IMPACT XPOZURES

Poinsettia

Poinsettia plants at Christmas have always been one of favorite decorations of the season, so when I saw an opportunity to hook a poinsettia rug, I jumped at the chance.

The *Poinsettia* rug I chose to hook was designed by Capri Boyle Jones. I began this rug with Capri at the Manistee Rug Camp in 2013. There were several challenges for me as I hooked.

To begin with, the design was a challenge, because it was the first time that I hooked one motif that was the entire rug. I usually hook a design that has many elements in it.

Another challenge was to look at the wool I chose from Capri in terms of values, not colors. If you look carefully at the poinsettia, you will see that there are several lay-ers. Capri helped me identify the layers from the top light layer down to the bottom dark layer. I used a variety of spot-dyed oranges, lavenders, and reds of different values. There were also several overdyed textures. Since a value is relative to the value next to it, I had to be very careful to read the values accurately. I had to make sure that I placed the values correctly from the light layer on top down to the dark layer. I hooked using a #6 cut.

In hooking each bract—the name for the leaves—I first hooked a broken line of lavender down the center to act as a vein. I then chose my wool. I hooked one side of the bract and then moved to the other side.

After hooking the salmon-colored bracts, I hooked several green bracts on the bottom. This is what one would see on an actual poinsettia plant. To show the buds in the center of the design, I used a fun glitzy yarn. With Capri's help I chose a spot-dyed greenish-gold wool for the border. All the wool that I used was dyed by Capri.

A major decision I had to make was to either finish the rug in the round or finish with the points. Of course it would have been so much easier for me just to make it round, but I decided I needed another challenge; I finished it using the points. I whipped the edges with yarn. I had to be very careful to cover the points with the yarn, so none of the backing showed through. It wasn't hard, just a little time consuming.

I really enjoyed hooking this rug. My *Poinsettia* rug will make a beautiful table topper during the Christmas season.

Poinsettia, 36" diameter, #6-cut hand-dyed wool and novelty yarn on rug warp.
Designed by Capri Boyle Jones and hooked by Susan Minorini, Lake Bluff, Illinois, 2015. KATHLEEN WEINSTEIN

Susan Minorini
Lake Bluff, Illinois

I began hooking in 1994. I love all widths, although it seems that I'm hooking with wider widths lately. I am a McGown Certified Instructor and, at present, president of the National Guild of Pearl K. McGown Hookrafters. I am the former assistant director of the McGown Teachers' Workshop Northern Division in Massachusetts. The Poinsettia rug is my second rug to appear in Celebration.

Exciting use of unexpected colors in the petals creates a show-stopper with depth and clarity; pointed edge difficult, dramatic, and finished perfectly. Great use of hooking direction to create vivacity and energy.

The Vine

Approximately ten years ago I saw this rug hooked by its designer, Capri Boyle Jones. The variety of colors in the beautiful, oversized, round shapes of the grapes spoke to me. That was truly an inspiration for me. Recently, I was given the opportunity to take a workshop with Capri as my teacher. Needless to say, I knew what I wanted to learn from her—how to hook those luscious grapes.

Capri provided most of the wool for this rug, mainly 3" x 12" strips of various dyed wools. Some of the wool is spot dyed, some overdyed and some as-is textures in a multitude of colors and values. As with other rug hookers, I would go to my stash as needed to supplement the color or for that just-right special accent.

The challenge for me was to create each grape in my choice of colors and values in order to produce a three-dimensional quality to the cluster of grapes. To create this illusion, I chose groupings of lighter value colors for the foremost grapes, with medium to darker values for the more distant grapes in each bunch. Each grape has its own character, and when I completed one grape, I was inspired to create the one next to it. Hooking the juicy grapes turned out to be a very rewarding experience.

After most of the grapes were complete, I hooked the rough, gnarly vine as a contrast to the smooth, round, opulent grapes. This vine had to appear to be strong and mature enough to hold the heavy clusters of grapes.

I hooked the leaves with a free-flowing movement, as though to hold the grapes in their more rigid space. The tendrils were almost whimsical in their curves and loops. I also used the tendrils as inspiration for the background in *The Vine*.

The Vine is bordered with dark gold—the

same textured wool used for a portion of the background. I tore the darker stripe from the same piece of wool so that it would make a comfortably contrasting border.

I whipped the edge with yarn to match the border, making the whipping more discreet. I used wool instead of rug tape to face the back of the rug. As previously, I tore

strips from the already-used textured wool and then hand sewed the wool to the back of the rug.

I had wanted to hook this rug for many years. I enjoyed hooking every grape and am pleased with the results. This rug hangs over our bed, where I enjoy seeing it every day.

Judith Rippstein
Fredericksburg, Texas

I moved to Fredericksburg in 1999 and went, as a visitor, to a hook-in; there I saw the fiber art of rug hooking for the first time. I quickly realized that I wanted to learn how to hook rugs. I found a teacher and completed my first rug in 2001. Since then, my work has appeared in Celebration *several times. Rug hooking is always a pleasure. It is my reward at the end of a busy day.*

In The Judges' Eyes

Visual power achieved by mixing cool and hot colors and values; curlicue background provides just enough shadow to anchor the grapes. Neat and precise binding; each grape plump and ready to pick; leaves hooked beautifully.

The Vine, 44" x 32", #5- to 7-cut wool on linen.
Designed by Capri Boyle Jones and hooked by Judith Rippstein, Fredericksburg, Texas, 2015. WHITE OAK STUDIOS

Zen Doodle

Zen Doodle, designed by Jane McGown Flynn, was slated to be taught at the 2014 McGown Teachers Workshop, Western Division, by our director, Michele Wise, a teacher highly regarded for her use of embellishments and innovation. To get started, I selected from her stash three mirrors (yes, actual mirrors), a purple sparkle dip dye and a dip dye that progressed from yellow through to red.

After returning home, I dug out my own stash of five brightly triped Dorr ombre wools—my latest absolute favorite wool to hook with. My preferred method of using ombre wools is to cut and hook them in order, dividing out the color segments and separating them with a thin line of black (#3-cut strip) to help make the colors really pop. I intermixed brightly colored plain hand-dyed wools with the ombre textures at a ratio of one plain to either two or three ombre textures per element.

I am not a rug hooker who shuns the use of pure white or black in my hooking—or any color for that matter. My color mantra is, "No color stands alone," because colors are like chameleons; they change, depending on what is placed around them.

Of late, I have also enjoyed exploring the use of very dark borders overlaying lighter interiors to heighten the feeling of depth.

At that same 2014 workshop, Lynne Powell taught her Zentangle® design in all black and white. I liked the contrast so decided to try hooking my interior in white and black. I was pleased with the effect.

I was sad when I pulled the last loop on this pillow top. This design is tailor-made to have fun with color. I am eager to do another!

Lynne M. Howard
Calgary, Alberta, Canada

Lynne began rug hooking in 1986 and is an active member of the Chinook Guild of Fibre Arts, Calgary, Alberta. She became a McGown Certified Instructor in the mid-1990s and has enjoyed teaching throughout western Canada, the western United States, Mexico, and in her home studio. Lynne finds rug hooking as exciting and engaging today as she did 30 years ago. Color planning, dyeing wool, and the friendship and inspiration she gets from other rug hookers are among her favorite aspects of this creative pastime. This is the third time Lynne's work has appeared in Celebration.

Zen Doodle, 19" square, #3- to 4-cut hand-dyed and Dorr ombre wool on linen.
Designed by Jane McGown Flynn and hooked by Lynne M. Howard, Calgary, Alberta, Canada, 2015. ALEX YONGE

In The Judges' Eyes

Ombre sections mixed with black make for a thrilling combo; nice, bold graphic contrast; excellent work using wool as-is and creating strong lines.

Barnwood

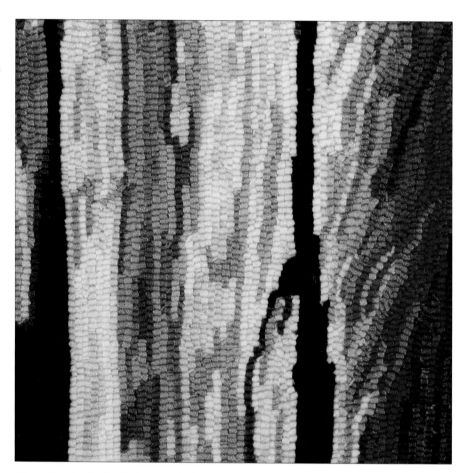

I was teaching a pictorial class at the Ragg Tyme School in Niagara-on-the-Lake, Ontario, when a student shared an art book, *Painting Weathered Buildings in Pen, Ink and Watercolor*, by Claudia Nice. My preference is fine cuts and especially pictorials; I fell in love with the illustrations throughout the pages of this book and immediately ordered a copy for myself. When I continually found myself going back to the same pages, reinspired by the same illustrations, I decided I wanted to hook *Barnwood*. After receiving permission to duplicate this illustration in our medium of rug hooking, my journey began.

First, I wanted to enlarge the overall size of the original piece. Using the grid system allowed me to increase the size of the original artwork, adding details block by block to get the results I wanted. I then began gathering and dyeing the wools I would need. Since I was already scheduled to attend a weekend retreat hosted by the Buckeye Rug Hooking Guild, I decided this is where I would start hooking *Barnwood*.

Although I had gathered a number of beautiful wools, I soon discovered—with the aid of the teacher, Karen Poetzinger—that I had gathered more dark wools and not enough light ones. A few purchases later, I was armed with Karen's lighter wools, my original wool stash, and a gray-scale approach to duplicating this piece. I began by hooking the hinge, then approached the boards, plank by plank. The last board on the right side proved to be the most challenging. Although it is overall slightly darker and contains more brown, when I hooked it the first time, it was visually too dark and didn't relate to the other planks. I ripped out some of the medium shades and replaced them with lighter ones. Although

this worked for the hooked piece, this board is not as true as the others to the original art.

Hooking on this project has taught me to look at objects differently. Instead of seeing something as a whole, I am now looking at the details. During a trip to New Orleans I found myself photographing close-up views—no doubt inspired from the pages of the *Weathered Buildings* book and my experience hooking *Barnwood*! The ferns growing from the cracked mortar of the

brick walls of the Lafayette Cemetery, or the skinny hinge secured with square nails that adorned a door revealing multiple layers of paint . . . perhaps one of these will be my next rug-hooking challenge.

It's interesting how just one chance encounter can send you in a different creative direction. A special thank-you to Laura Boszormeny for introducing me to the wonderful book, *Painting Weathered Buildings*.

Linda K. Powell
Navarre, Ohio

Linda is a McGown Certified Instructor and is the current director for the Southern McGown Teachers Workshop. She is a member of ATHA, the National Guild of Pearl K. McGown Hookrafters, and the Ontario Hooking Craft Guild, currently participating in the OHCG teacher training program. Linda teaches classes in her home studio, at local venues, and at workshops. This is her second appearance in Celebration. Her rug Gartenstraße (Garden Street) *appeared in Celebrations XXV.*

Barnwood, 23" x 17½", #4-cut hand-dyed wool on rug warp.
Adapted with permission and hooked by Linda K. Powell, Navarre, Ohio, 2015. Glenn Kerns

Judicious use of white and black really make this piece pop; can practically hear that hinge squeak! Very painterly, good depth and great "old wood and metal" feel. Captures the essence of barn wood: the wood, weathered; the hinge, rusty; colors work well to express this.

Basking Ridge Floral

My inspiration for *Basking Ridge Floral* began at a resale shop, where I spotted a plaque with an appealing design. After looking at it more closely, I found a label on the back describing its history. I was surprised to learn that it was actually an etching of a 1760 gravestone from a cemetery in Basking Ridge, New Jersey. I thought that, with some modifications, it would make an interesting design for a hooked rug.

I made the purchase and put it in my wool room, where it sat until I signed up for a "Design Your Own Rug" class with Susan Feller. I thought this would be the perfect time to use that idea for a rug. After playing around with different adaptations of the design, and with input from Susan, I came up with a pattern I was happy with.

I had a good friend who was in the process of trying to downsize her wool stash and didn't know what to do with her leftover worms from various projects. I told her to throw them in my basket, and I would sort through them for use in this project. She was happy to be rid of them, and I was happy she had donated them to me—I just loved the mixture of her colors.

I had so much fun pulling her different wools from the basket and hooking them into the floral and border parts of the pattern. The only problem was that she used mostly #8 and wider cuts, while I used mostly #6 cuts. So, I had to hand cut most of her worms to make them work in my piece.

I got the idea for the striped background from one of Susan Feller's rugs that she brought to class. In order for me to keep the lines straight, I drew lines on the linen, which proved to be very helpful. On my striped background, I used a mixture of wool off the bolt and hand dyed. The edge of the

rug is finished with a piece of hand-dyed wool cut on the bias and hand sewn into place.

I had some sad news about a month after returning from class. My kind friend who had given me the wonderful worms had

passed away. As I finished hooking the rug with her worms, I thought of all the happy times we had together.

This rug will always be a fond memory of my special friend.

Jill Hicks
Valparaiso, Indiana

My introduction to rug hooking began about six years ago when my husband gave me the Christmas gift of a class at the Green Mountain Rug Hooking School. The experience was wonderful, and I became thoroughly hooked. Basking Ridge Floral is my second rug to be featured in Celebration.

Basking Ridge Floral, 21½" x 41", #6- and hand-cut wool on linen. Adopted from a 1760 gravestone in a Basking Ridge, New Jersey, cemetery and hooked by Jill Hicks, Valparaiso, Indiana, 2014. JAYME GOETZ

Cougar Close Up

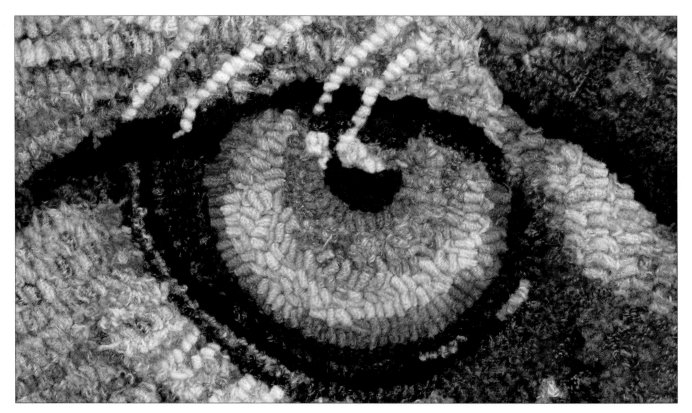

After hooking many fine-cut realistic animals, it was time to take a walk on the wild side and try something different. A wide-cut realistic animal.

I chose *Cougar Close Up* after seeing the photo on Facebook. The eyes spoke to me and kept pulling me back for another look. Not only was the photo beautiful, it was taken at an animal sanctuary that I visit at least once a year. I obtained permission to use the photo and I was off on my wide cut adventure. This wide cut would challenge me and also show you can mix wools and create realism with wide cuts.

The eyes are #6, the whiskers #4, and the remainder of the piece is hooked with #8. The eyes are my favorite part of the rug and combined as-is and textured wool to create the depth and realism I saw in the photo. It was so much fun to look through my reducer and see the cougar looking back at me! When looking at this rug from a distance, the eyes pull you in, just as the photo pulled me in on Facebook.

The biggest challenge, for me, was having to "think big" to translate my 5" x 7" photo into a 20" x 26" rug. By looking closely at the details and filling one area at a time, I was able to translate what I saw in the photo.

The hooking progressed quickly, and I had as much fun mixing wools with the #8 cut as I do with a #4 cut. I used some dyed wool, but the majority of the piece is hooked with over 50 different textures. A little of this wool, and a little of that wool, create realistic color and value changes in the fur. The spots and value changes in the nose make you want to reach out and touch it.

Cougar Close Up was my first wide-cut realistic animal, but it will not be my last. I continue to take and gather photos as I look for my next subject.

Judy A. Carter
Willow Street, Pennsylvania

Judy is a Master Artisan with the Pennsylvania Guild of Craftsmen and a McGown Certified Instructor. This is her thirteenth time in Celebration; she was a Featured Exhibit at Sauder Village in 2015. Judy is the author of the book Hooking Animals.

Cougar Close Up, 20" x 26", #4-, 6-, and 8-cut hand-dyed and as-is wool on monk's cloth.
Adapted with permission from a photograph by Lunasa Photography (Louise Higgins) and
hooked by Judy A. Carter, Willow Street, Pennsylvania, 2015.

Dick and Francie

Ann Sale is my first cousin, Dick is her husband, and Francie is their dog. Ann and I grew up together in Richmond, Virginia. We have always been close in spirit if not in where we lived. We have kept in touch through all the years since our childhood. Recently she wrote that they had acquired a new dog, so I asked her to send me a photo of her.

When I received Ann's picture of Dick and Francie, I knew that I wanted to hook it! It was such a lovely portrait with the sunny background, Dick wearing his elegant hat and reading the paper, while Francie snuggled close to him. I didn't tell Ann of my plans because I didn't know how it would turn out. So I surprised them with it (it wasn't quite completed) when we gathered for a family event. They were so happy with it that I suggested that my "pay" would be for them to come for a visit when it was finished. The best reward that I could possibly imagine for the hooking was to have several wonderful visits with them after not seeing them for so many years. Ann had told me that Dick was not in good health, so when we lost him in December, I was especially appreciative that the hooking had brought us back together.

Laura Pierce was my teacher for the portrait at the Cambria Pines Rug School in California. She is an expert with hooking faces and has helped me with a number of projects. First, it is important to have good flesh tones, at least a light, medium, and dark. Laura also challenges her students to use a variety of colors instead of black, but in the same value, when shading—such as purple, blue, or green. It is also essential to have a good drawing of the face to get the features correctly placed: eyes, nose, mouth, and ears.

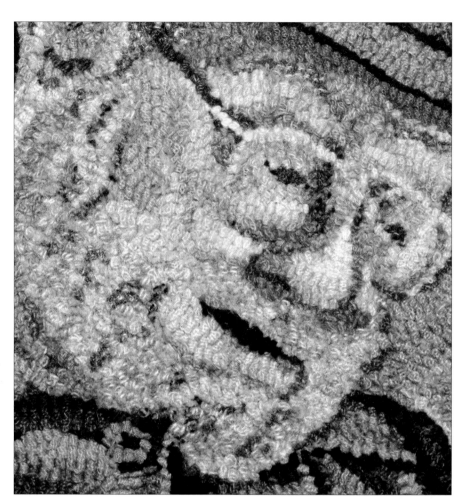

I start with the shadows and highlights, and then fill in with the middle values. When copying a photograph, I usually make a blow-up the same size as my hooking and trace that on the linen with Red Dot Tracing Material.

I enjoyed hooking the blue shirt because I like to hook clothing. The eyeglasses were probably the most difficult. I have hooked quite a few dogs, so Francie was fun. Here again, I used some purple-grays instead of black in her fur for shading. I struggled a bit to find the right wool for the sunny light in the background, but I think that what I found adds vigor to the portrait. I collect wool from various teachers and sources as I travel for workshops so I have a large stash from my many years of hooking.

Sarah Province
Silver Spring, Maryland

Fiber art in the form of rug hooking has been my creative outlet and delight for 48 years. As an artist, I love the freedom of the hooked process that can be unhooked when an adjustment or correction needs to be made. The hunt for just the right color in the wool fabric is as creative as mixing the palette for a watercolor. This is my thirteenth rug to appear in Celebration.

In The Judges' Eyes

Dick's hat and facial features particularly well done. Nice shading on the face; good use of colors. Artist expressed great love and caring between man and dog; face is done beautifully.

Dick and Francie, 16" x 21", #3- and 4-cut wool on linen.
Adapted with permission from a photograph by Ann Sale and hooked by Sarah Province,
Silver Spring, Maryland, 2014. LLOYD ATOR

Eagle Spirit

In May of 2015, my annual rug-hooking treat, Caraway Rug School in Sophia, North Carolina, was fast approaching and I hadn't yet decided on a pattern! I was considering another adaptation of an impressionist painting, an original design, or ordering a pattern from one of my catalogs, when a thought occurred to me. A few years ago I saw a greeting card designed by artist Jody Bergsma. After requesting a catalog and obtaining her permission, I hooked *Dream*, which appeared in *Celebration XXIII*. I really liked the way *Dream* turned out, so I selected another Jody Bergsma design from the catalog for my camp project. "Eagle Spirit Come...and inspire us to fly" was a perfect selection and challenge.

After obtaining permission from Jody Bergsma, I enlarged the picture, traced it on Red Dot Tracing Material, then transferred it to my rug-warp backing. Of course, like all rug hookers, I have a lot of leftover wool that I had dyed for previous projects. I was determined to use some of this "stash" for *Eagle Spirit*. I selected various shades of gray, white, black, gold, brown, and, of course, my favorite on the color wheel—orange. I was finally ready for rug camp!

Since the eagles' eyes were the focal point of the design, I hooked them first. My teacher, Diane Stoffel, helped me capture the intense look in their eyes. All the eagles were hooked with stronger rust and brown colors using #3- and 4-cut spot-dyed 100% Dorr wool. For the head feathers on two of those eagles I used natural, white, and pale gray wool. The Native American Thunderbird, symbolizing strength and spirit, was hooked using #5 and #6 cuts. To get a soft flowing effect for the background, I hooked directionally, using only grays and tans in a # 6 cut. Outlining in black makes your eye

travel around the rug and intensifies the eagles.

The border is an as-is Wool Studio brown, rust, and gold plaid in a #6 cut. After

about a month of hooking, the steamed and bound *Eagle Spirit* was done—a fun and inspiring piece to hook!

Karen Whidden
Southern Pines, North Carolina

I began rug hooking in 2003 and have hooked almost 200 pieces, both primitive and finely shaded. Dyeing my own wool is both relaxing and creative. My rugs have appeared in the ATHA magazine and Rug Hooking magazine's Celebration of Hand-Hooked Rugs.

In The Judges' Eyes

Delicacy of the white feather a great counterpoint to three such intimidating birds. Fabulous eyes pull you right into the rug; strong medicine in this spiritual piece. Border well chosen to play off the main characters; birds intermingle so well.

Eagle Spirit, 16" x 22", #2-, 4-, and 6-cut wool on rug warp.
Adapted with permission from original artwork by Jody Bergsma and hooked by Karen Whidden,
Southern Pines, North Carolina, 2015. JOHN WHIDDEN

Elena Marie

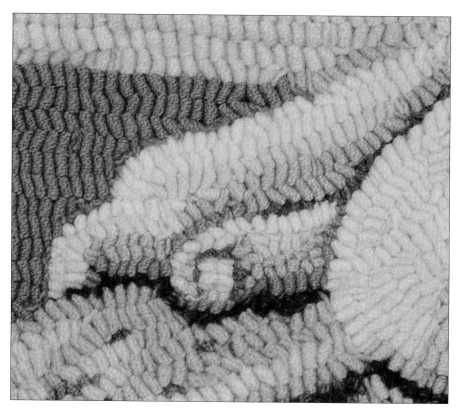

In September 2014, my husband and I were privileged to have Gene Shepherd come to Riverhouse Inn & Cottages to teach a three-day workshop. While teaching here, he encouraged his students to come to his "1st Annual California Getaway" the following January at his home studio in Anaheim. I booked my flights.

Before settling on the piece that I would work on with Gene (I was tempted to just be lazy and do something simple that took no thought, but what a waste of a great teacher!), I asked him what he thought of my doing a portrait in a wide cut. I had never done a portrait before, and I don't know that he had either, but he wasn't fazed.

The previous summer, I had received a copy of a photo that was taken of my granddaughter, Elena, by her Nana Hall. Elena had been playing at a park and had stopped to look at something that caught her attention. She looked like she was lost in thought, and the image struck me as something that I would like to someday capture in wool.

Gene agreed to dye the wool that I would need for my project and, though I do my own dyeing most of the time, I was happy to have him do it. I did bring mottled green for the background and the wool for the railing. He also suggested that I get the photo copied in various shades of black and white and a full-color photo to have as visuals.

The first few days of hooking involved getting the facial features set. Her nose, eye, and ear were crucial to making this look like Elena. So much "putting in" and "pulling out"! It looked awful, and I was not sure that I was going to be able to ever get it to look like my granddaughter. I wondered what I had gotten myself into.

I took many photos as I worked each day,

a way of stepping back to see my progress. The beginning photos are not pretty! Sometimes I show them to people who see the finished work and say that they could never hook anything like this. They are speechless when they see how it started off. If I can hook a portrait, anyone can!

I created a good likeness with *much* tweaking (four hours to get her thumb to the point that I was satisfied with it), stepping back for a look, a pointer from Gene (okay, maybe more than one) and a love for the subject matter. It took me about two months to finish the rug.

This was the most difficult piece that

I've hooked to date because it had to look like a particular person and not just "a" person. *Elena Marie* has also been my most rewarding work. My husband laid claim to it before it was even finished. This to me was great affirmation that it looked like our granddaughter.

When I showed the completed rug to five-year-old Elena, she asked if it was for her. While hooking it, I hadn't decided who the recipient would be. Since my husband claimed it first, I told her that the rug would be hers when Grandpa was finished with it. Happily, she was okay with that answer and didn't ask when that would be!

Sue-Anne Jay
Montague, Prince Edward Island, Canada

In 2005, I took a beginners' class using an antique-style hooking frame and hand cutting my strips. I completed three rugs that first year. After investing in a lap frame and a Bliss cutter, I thought I was in heaven. I've now graduated to a Townsend floor frame and Townsend cutter (Let the angels sing!). I always have something on my frame and my favorite project is my next one!

In The Judges' Eyes

A master class on the successful interplay of light and shadow; technical skills are particularly fine. Nice skin tones and shading of hair; strong lights and darks make for drama.

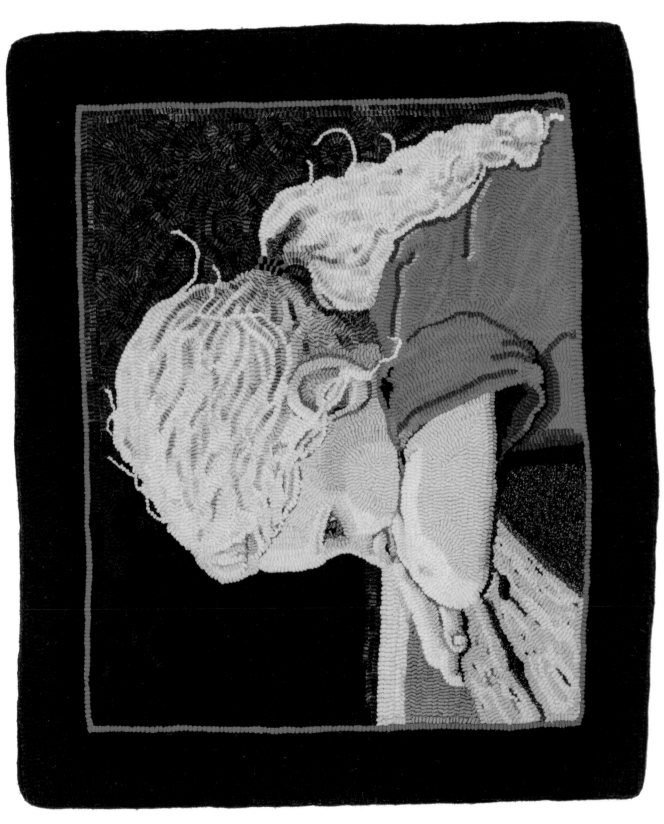

Elena Marie, 24" x 21", #3- to 6-cut hand-dyed wool on linen. Adapted with permission from a photograph by Andrea Hall and hooked by Sue-Anne Jay, Montague, Prince Edward Island, Canada, 2015. DAN MacKINNON

Floravians

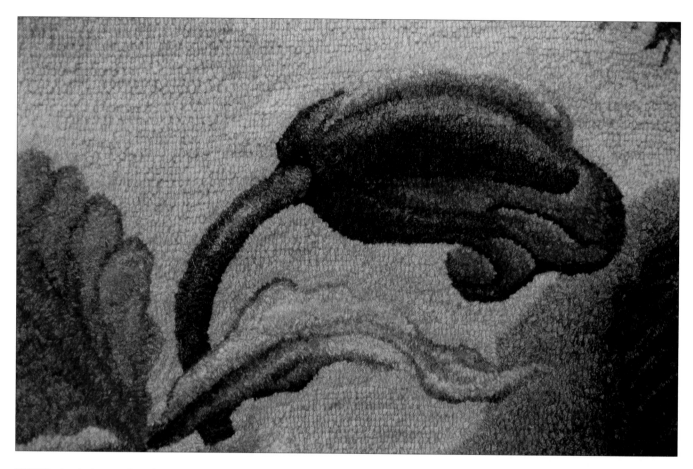

To hook this rug, I used nine swatches from four different dye formulas; five are transitional swatches. When hooked together, the colors provided a wide variety of chromas and hues, producing natural looking petals.

Transitional swatches always blend harmoniously with their base swatch and add subtle variations to the overall look. These swatches are prepared in the same way as a regular swatch, but two different dye formulas are added to each jar. One is the regular swatch formula and different amounts of this dye are added to each jar; the other dye formula is a much weaker dye solution containing a single dye. The same amount of this second dye is added to each jar.

Think of a transitional swatch as a regular swatch dyed over a pastel-colored wool. The color mix is the individual rug hooker's choice. I use transitional swatches everywhere because they add so much flexibility.

My swatches were 10-value swatches. The two values lighter than 1—0 and 00—are useful when fine shading pastel areas (such as an orchid petal) or water or snow scenes. These 2 values are obtained by reducing the dye concentrate of its darker companion by half; for example, if, for value 1, I used ½ tsp. of dye concentrate, then for value 0, I would use ¼ tsp., and ⅛ tsp. for value 00.

Roland Nunn
Clayton, California

A familiar presence in Celebration, Roland has hooked all types of rugs: geometric, Oriental, floral, animals, landscapes, and scrolls. His source material is wide-ranging, and he uses calendar photos and greeting cards. He has received numerous awards, including best of show, at the Alameda County Fair in Pleasanton, California. This is his eleventh rug to appear in Celebration.

Love the pop of color in throat of orchid; hummingbirds glow like little gems! Beautifully formed loops with wonderful precision; movement of birds echoed in movement of flowers. Glow in colors contrasts with serenity of background.

Floravians, 23" x 31", #3-cut wool in 10-value swatches on monk's cloth.
Adapted from a painting by Martin Johnson Heade and hooked by Roland Nunn, Clayton, California, 2013. SCOTT MCCUE

Greta Garbo

I enjoy creating both original designs and adaptations in my rug hooking. The painting of Greta Garbo spoke to me from the first time I saw it, but it was many months before I actually started. The image rolled around in my head during that time, and I think that subconsciously my brain was trying to figure out how to do it, as I had never attempted a portrait before. And then one day I just started—and from that day until the day it was completed I just could not put it down. I became obsessed with trying to bring Greta to life with wool!

The first step was to decide what backing to use. I had used linen in the past, but it was too soft for my liking; I found some good-quality burlap that provided the stiffness that I prefer in a backing material. The next step was to decide what size I wanted the final rug to be so it would be large enough to hook the level of detail I wanted. Once the outside dimensions were drawn, it was a matter of drawing the portrait—which was challenging but really fun.

I then had to find the right colors, textures, and thicknesses of wool. Some I had in my stash, but for the rest I made a trip to vendors in Maine to find what I needed. Some yarns are 3-ply of various textures and weights, and others are 3-ply unraveled to 2- or 1-ply. I started hooking parts of the clothing and hat just to get a feel for it, but then I knew I had to do the eye— because if I couldn't do the eye, I couldn't do the rug. One of the things I found most interesting about the eye (I had never hooked an eye before) was that it seemed to come alive when I added the tiniest little flecks of one of the turquoise blues to the iris. Once the eye was done, it was as if Greta were watching my every move; from then on, her eye followed me everywhere!

After the eye, I tackled the lips and then went back and finished the hat and clothing and hair. The skin tones were challenging, especially finding the right colors. But I love the subtle contrast between the 2 sides of the face, one side in the light and the other in the shade! The finished rug was framed with a simple gold-colored wooden frame.

Susan J. Baker
Stanbridge East, Quebec, Canada

I discovered rug hooking at an Upper Canada Village demonstration in 2010. I started out hooking with hand-cut wool strips, but even using a cutter was frustrating because of fraying fabric and uneven strips. I was introduced to hooking with wool yarn by one of the Brome County Rug Hookers, and ever since have been "hooked" on yarn. Greta Garbo is my first portrait and my first submission to Celebration. *What a thrill to be selected as a finalist!*

In The Judges' Eyes

You had me with the eye and lips; what a strong interpretation. Wow! Great strength in design and colors; says "Stop and look at me."

Greta Garbo, 20¾" x 26½", wool yarn of various textures and weights, some hand dyed and some hand spun, on burlap. Adapted with permission from a painting by Canadian artist Kim Hunter and hooked by Susan J. Baker, Stanbridge East, Quebec, Canada, 2014. KAREN SMITH

Home Sweet Home

The inspiration for my rug came from an old paint store pamphlet from the 1930s I found in an antique shop. I loved the simple graphic look of the cover picture.

I was getting ready to go to the Heirloom Rug School in Holland, Michigan. I decided this was the project I wanted to start on. I drew out my pattern and transferred it to Scottish burlap, which is my preferred backing. The tighter weave allows me to hook in small details with the narrow cuts.

I asked my teacher, Katie Puckett, to dye the wool for this rug. I wanted simple, basic color—red, yellow, blue, green, black, and white. You will see the same blue in the sky as in the shading on the fence. To add depth to the piece I used black in the trees, which helped to make the house stand out. Black also serves in the shading of the bushes and other smaller areas.

I used a #2 cut and even trimmed those strips a little to hook the furniture in the front of the house. There are a few more #2 cuts in other areas, then #3 and #4 cuts for the rest of the rug. I did not hook a border: I finished the rug with the wool fabric instead of rug binding. This was the easiest, most fun—and least stressful—rug I have ever hooked.

I was introduced to rug hooking about 25 years ago from a *Country Living* magazine picture of beautiful hooked rugs stretched over an old wooden fence. I knew right then I had to try this art form. I discovered and started attending a rug school in Decorah, Iowa, and joined a group of rug hookers in Newton that I still hook with every week. I became a McGown Certified Instructor at North Central McGown Teachers Workshop, where I have also taught.

Joanne Thomason
Newton, Iowa

I have a studio at The Centre for Arts and Artists in Newton, where I display my rugs and teach classes. My rugs have been published in two of Jessie Turbayne's books: my art deco Dream Girl *in* The Creative Hooker *and Van Gogh's Café* Terrace at Night *in* Hooked On Rugs. *I was honored to have a rug on the cover of the September/October 2008 issue of* Rug Hooking *magazine. I am a member of ATHA and Central Iowa Rug Artists Guild. This is the first time I have submitted a rug for* Celebration.

In The Judges' Eyes

Very precise hooking; bold graphics and stylized design of a vintage travel poster. Great graphic rendering; strong use of color and strong, compelling statement.

Home Sweet Home, 34" x 20", #2- to 4-cut wool on Scottish burlap.
Adapted from a circa 1930s store pamphlet and hooked by Joanne Thomason, Newton, Iowa, 2015. JOHN LEE

Hungry Animals Alphabet

A display of a small crib quilt top at a local quilt store caught my attention. The pattern had 20 squares of exquisitely detailed whimsical animals, all of which were associated with food. Each of the 20 squares represented a letter or two of the alphabet and an animal that began with each of the letters. The creative wheels started turning, and I was adapting it in my mind's eye to a rug or wall hanging. I purchased the pattern and couldn't wait to contact the artist.

Janet Wecker-Frisch is the artist who designed a fabric line of *Hungry Animals Alphabet* characters featured in a fabric collection created for South Sea Imports. I was able to contact her via email and later had the privilege to speak with her by phone in Missouri. She very generously granted me permission to adapt her images for a rug or wall hanging.

The first challenge was to enlarge a roughly 38" x 30" pattern with 7" x 7" squares to rug size. I eventually settled on 8½" x 9" squares with ¾" separating lines. I took the traced 7" x 7" squares to a copy service and had them enlarge the squares to size.

The next challenge was to transfer the pattern to a backing. After tracing the enlarged pattern on Red Dot Tracing Material, I began the process of tracing it *again* on rug warp. The whole enlarging and transfer process took three weeks.

Once I started hooking, it was critical to make sure that all the lines separating the squares were properly aligned both horizontally and vertically while maintaining the size integrity of each square. After the first row, it was easier to tweak the squares to fit when it was needed.

The artist had done the color planning,

and I was able to use wool I had on hand for most of it—only dyeing some small pieces for the different skies. The red wool for the separating lines was dyed for me by Loris Blandford (The Wool Farm) and came as close to Janet's red as humanly possible. Each square was its own little picture, so it held my interest from start to finish. I like learning to use different techniques and materials, especially the use of embellishments. It was great fun to embellish with

beads (I sacrificed a necklace), yarn, and a bit of ribbon.

It was impossible to duplicate with a #3 cut the detail in the original artwork, which I believe was in watercolor. But I tried to stay as true as possible to the original. If ever there was a project I didn't want to end, it was this one. The crib top has been quilted, and it and the rug make an interesting pair.

Betty Burbage
Berlin, Maryland

About 22 years ago, I saw Janice Russell demonstrating rug hooking at a local 19th century restored village. I currently serve as president of Delmarva Friendship Rugcrafters and am inspired by and learn from the variety of rugs our members produce. I am lucky to have two schools in my backyard, April School at Dunes Manor, in Ocean City, and November Workshop at the same location. I attend these every year to catch up with sister "hookers" and to learn from the skilled teachers there.

Amazing attention to detail in each block and every single motif; each block a perfect little gem. Nostalgic and playful; so well executed with all that detail. What whimsy! What fun!

Hungry Animals Alphabet, 49½" x 41", #3- and 4-cut wool, beads, and ribbon on rug warp. Adapted with permission from a quilt design by Janet Wecker-Frisch and hooked by Betty Burbage, Berlin, Maryland, 2014. BETTY MASTERS

Japanese Mosaic

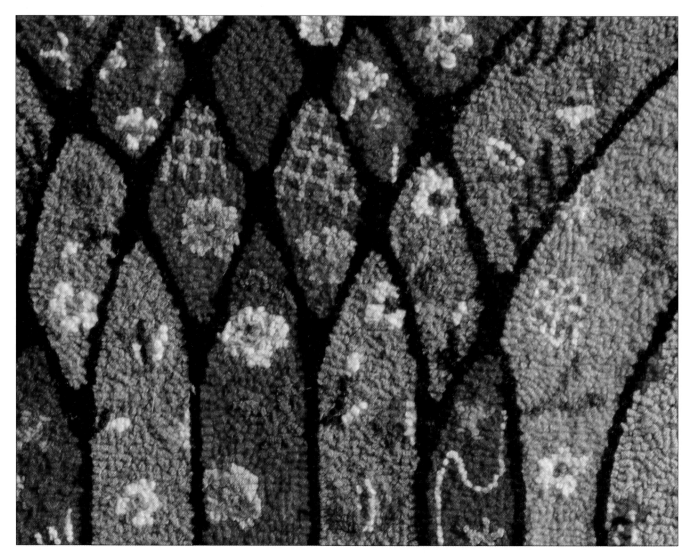

At first sight, Kitty Pippen's quilt originally titled *Japanese Silk Mosaic* fascinated me. I was intrigued by the geometric design and the beautiful Japanese silk material used to quilt it. Originally, I was going to hook the different sections in solid colors; then I had the idea of trying to re-create the effect of fabric. This decision was also the most difficult aspect of the piece: It was necessary to achieve a balance of background and flowers so that the geometric nature of the quilt was not lost, but at the same time to create designs and use colors that suggested different pieces of material.

I dyed all the wool myself except for the inner light yellow, which was a gift from rug hooking friend Cathy Oomen, and the outer gold, which was a lovely abrashed piece purchased from Martina Lesar's Hooked Rug Studio. I dip dyed, spot dyed, and dyed solid colors over new Dorr wool as well as using leftover swatches from other rugs. The formulae I used were Carolyn Clemens's Jewel Tones and ones from Christine Little's Majic Carpet Dyes books.

All the flowers and leaves were hooked in #2 and 3 cuts; I purchased a #2 Fraser cutter especially for the rug. With the abrashed outer gold and the coral spot-dye at the corners, I cut the wool and taped the strips to cardboard as it was cut. I then hooked the strips in sequence, trying to pool the colors to achieve a mottled, abrashed effect.

Hooking the piece was a lot of fun as it combined the two things I enjoy hooking most: geometrics and flowers. In doing this piece, I gained a new respect for fabric designers. Creating the designs of the individual sections was the most challenging part of this project.

To finish the rug, I had it mounted on stretcher bars. It now hangs in my living room, where it replaced a painting that used to hang in that spot. (I gave the painting to one of my daughters and kept the rug.)

Japanese Mosaic, 23" square, #2- to 4-cut wool on traditional linen.
Adapted with permission from a quilt design by Kitty Pippen and hooked by Susan Grant,

Susan Grant
Georgetown, Ontario, Canada

I started hooking rugs in 2004 when I retired from teaching. Japanese Mosaic is my third rug to be featured in Celebration. In total I have competed about 15 rugs; I have also hooked an assortment of pillows, Christmas stockings, table mats, and wall hangings.

In The Judges' Eyes

Amazing design detail; widening of the line joints give great weight to the curving lines. Eye-catching use of flower elements moving through the design; strong design and pleasant use of color.

Jesus of Nazareth

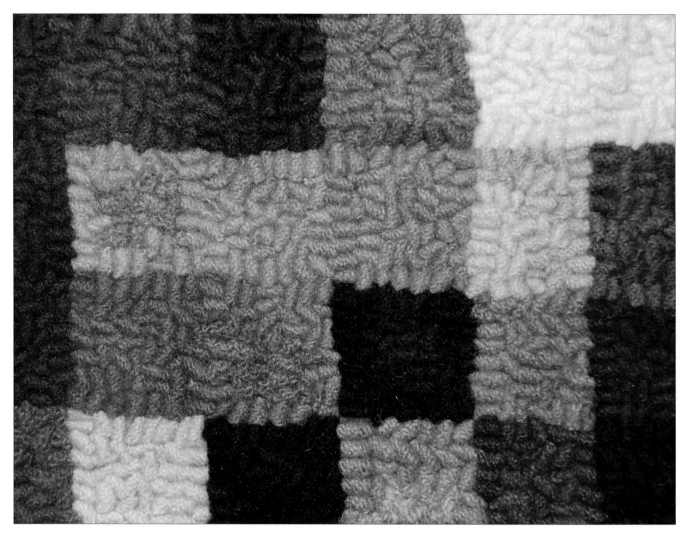

Every year I challenge myself as an artist, whether it is the scale of the rug I chose to hook, or the use of green in a portrait, or how moonlight is captured differently from sunlight. In 2015, I chose to focus on form or design. I wanted to break down a rug to its bare minimum in terms of form—literally to the square inch. So I turned to the most traditional rug we can hook, the inch mat. How could I break open this simple form so that it would do something inch mats usually don't do? Could I take what is a basic geometric design used for hit-or-miss and create a portrait in square inches?

I chose Jesus of Nazareth as my subject, obtaining copyright clearance to base my design on the famous crucifixion scene in the 1977 film *Jesus of Nazareth* where Robert Powell, as Jesus, suffers the crown of thorns. I was deeply affected by this scene as a young woman, and this image of Jesus will always be Jesus to me. I wanted to create this rug as a companion to the rug *Mary Magdalene* that I designed and hooked two years ago. My rug *Jesus of Nazareth* was created to hang on the wall of my office next to Mary.

Using a pixelated map of the original image as my guide, I hooked each inch square by its value (by the lightness or darkness of the color) with no regard for color. Each inch square, in fact, contains at least two different colors of the same value.

I had imagined a monochromic portrait, so I dyed 14 different colors in the rose-plum-brown spectrum, each in 8-value swatches. So the rug contains 112 different values of color, some bright colors and some duller.

My goal was to create a rug that ought to be viewed in person, because where you stand in proximity to the rug makes a difference in terms of what you actually see. The closer you get to the rug, the more you see only squares of color. The farther away you stand from the rug (the broader the view you have) the clearer your focus becomes, and you are able to see Jesus' face as if it were a photograph. There is a lesson here for me as a professor of early Christianity—that standing at a distance brings Jesus into better focus.

Jesus of Nazareth, 43" x 39", #6-cut hand-dyed new wool, in 14 different Red Jack Rugs 8-value packs, on linen. Adapted with permission from a photograph by NBC and hooked by April D. DeConick, Houston, Texas, 2015.

April D. DeConick
Houston, Texas

April is an award-winning hooked wool artist and master dyer. Her work has been featured in five editions of Celebration, *in* Rug Hooking *magazine, and in the ATHA Newsletter. Her rugs and dyed wool have received four People's Choice Awards at Sauder Village. The author of* The Wool Palette *and* Wool Snapshots, *April is president of the Stash Sisters ATHA Guild in Region 9. She began hooking in 1995 in rural Michigan. She is a professor of the New Testament and Early Christianity at Rice University, where she chairs the Department of Religion.*

The Dance of Life

My love of nature, birds, and flowers helped me find inspiration for creating this rug. I have hooked many types of herons but fell in love with the graceful egrets when visiting the South. Then, I found a photo of a white and a black egret—they looked like they were dancing. The positions of the birds spoke to me and led to the creation of this rug.

Once I find a subject I spend time researching details about the birds. This gives me insight into what else I will add to my piece; I added fish to this one. Through my research I also found that egrets symbolize patience, tranquility, resourcefulness, and transition, which were reflecting my state of being at that time.

At first, I thought the white egret would be the easiest to hook, but it was a challenge to get the right shades of gray into the white to create the form. By adding some light grays around the wing and neck, the body finally had a shape. I then hooked areas that I wanted to be higher in the Waldoboro technique. I sculpted them into the shapes that worked for the bird's wings and body. After many trimmings, along with adding more wool to fill and thicken the areas, I started hooking in yarns and other fibers to add texture.

The last step in hooking the egrets was adding the feathers. That's when the birds seem to come alive with their own personalities. I sewed the feathers with a heavy cord through the wool and linen; the cord is attached in the back. The yarns and feathers draw people to the birds, and they want to touch the birds to feel the different textures.

The final challenge was finding the best way to frame this piece. The edges tended to curl up more than on a flat piece, and the raised bird areas can't be blocked. I sewed

on a wool strip for the border and stretched it to a wood frame for more support and to prevent it from curling.

The art of weaving allowed me to work with different textures and fibers to create my pieces. When I realized that rug hooking could do the same thing, I knew I had found the right medium for me to continue creat-

ing. Experimenting with silks, velvets, shiny yarns, fuzzy yarns, and feathers gives a different look to my rug hooking and seems to bring life to my birds. I am looking forward to creating more interesting hooked birds, experimenting with new types of materials, and dyeing beautiful colors of wool.

Sandra Grant
Warren, Vermont

I had a successful weaving business for 25 years. Eight years ago, when I could no longer weave, I tried painting and other crafts. These led to a rug hooking class with Jackye Hansen on the Waldoboro technique. My interest was captivated, and I started creating birds and dyeing my own wool. The Dance of Life is my first rug to be featured in Celebration.

In The Judges' Eyes

Three-dimensional features really enhance this piece; creative use of yarns and feathers make bird come alive. Interesting surface; movement of birds makes them alive, moving toward us as the water moves backward.

The Dance of Life, 36" x 24", #3- and 4-cut dip-dyed and spot-dyed wools, feathers, and textured yarns on linen. Adapted from an unattributed photo and hooked by Sandra Grant, Warren, Vermont, 2015.

The Gleaners

Hooking *The Gleaners* has been on my bucket list since I saw it hooked at a Cream City Hook-in years ago. I saw many varied colorations of the original painting and went with this one because I liked the portrayal of light to dark moving across the piece.

I wanted to do the hooking in #8 and #8.5 cuts, along with hand-cut details, to prove shading can be done with wider cuts. It can when the picture is enlarged to this size. I have a large wool collection and was able to pick out most of the shades I needed; I had to dye only the sky and the dark ground wool.

I took one woman at a time and studied her dress folds. I saw so many colors the painter had incorporated into each outfit—it was fascinating. The adage rang true that it is about value and not so much about color: I used olive, blue, purple, and gray for one skirt.

I found it challenging to see so many colors in the clothing and not try to hook each stroke of the paintbrush. After all, my "brush" was a quarter-inch-wide strip of wool. I had to edit and simplify the painter's work.

The use of textures was so much fun, especially the bouclés I used in the ground. Splashing some dark indigo blue-black over red-brown was an easy way to portray that dark ground. The "painting" of light with wool was an interesting growth endeavor—straining to hook "shine" on the scarves and shoulders, while shadowing the necks and waists of the bent-over women.

In the end I did simplify the background and edit out one hand that was in the original painting but proved vexing to the portrait in wool. Actually, it did make the overall composition better.

Finally, I added some hand-cut details to accentuate outstretched hands and shoes under a dress, which added interest. When working on this rug, I definitely needed the natural light of daytime to get the colors right.

There were growing pains, but now I can check that one off the bucket list and move on!

Cathy Stephan
Athens, Wisconsin

I live on a farm in Central Wisconsin and have hooked for 20 years.
I teach at camps in the Midwest and hold workshops at my home studio.
I love primitives as well as the occasional challenge piece.

The Gleaners, 53" x 40", #8 and 8.5-cut wool with hand-cut details on linen. Adapted from a painting by Jean-François Millet and hooked by Cathy Stephan, Athens, Wisconsin, 2014. GALL PHOTOGRAPHY

In The Judges' Eyes

Single line of blue in the border brings all the colors together. Nice detail in the clothing; great sky; great color control. Wonderful adaptation; amazing what can be done with wide cut.

Women Rising

It was a chance encounter with Jeanne Field in the mid-1970s that opened up my world to rug hooking. We met in the back hooking room of Jeanne's Blue Willow Wool Shop while I was on the hunt for needlepoint tapestry wool. I became an avid hooker and student of Jeanne's—and of many of the other wonderful teachers available at the time. In the early 1990s, career pressures forced me to set hooking aside until the summer before my retirement in December 2008. I found a local group and returned to hooking the first week of January 2009.

I had pulled out unfinished projects to work on, but tastes can change over the years. I decided to thin out the long-kept stash and to work only on what pleased me now. And as I searched for new projects, I soon realized there was a new hooking

world out there: Not everything was #3 cut and shaded any more. I became excited as I began to explore larger cuts and the mixed media works I was seeing. I am a workshop junkie. My greatest joy comes from learning new methods from great teachers. The new friendships I have made—and the old ones I rekindled in the hooking world—have made this craft a total package for me.

Women Rising came out of a week-long workshop at the Trent School of Rug Hooking in Ontario. I decided to take an intriguing class on hooking kaleidoscopes that was being taught by Judy Kielczewski. I love the intricacy of kaleidoscopes, a complexity that demands vibrant colors. Judy's style of teaching was to encourage her students to be as creative as possible—then to challenge and stretch themselves even more. I researched the shapes and colors that appealed to me

and, during my research, kept returning to a piece of free clip art on the Internet that spoke to me. I enlarged the picture and transferred it to linen using Red Dot Tracing Material.

I color planned the rug from fragments of my own stash, with help from Ingrid Hieronimus, Shirley Lyons, and my good friend, Anne Boissinot. When I started hooking the piece, it just felt so right, even with #3, shading, and beading. I loved hooking this piece, and I always looked forward to picking it up and working on it. The finishing was a *déjà vu* moment for me because I brought it to the framer who had done all my needlepoint pieces over 40 years earlier. The original owner's son was now running the store and he too specialized in blocking fiber. His framing is just beautiful.

Women Rising, 28" octagon, #3-cut swatches, dip dye and mottled 100% wool on linen.
Adapted from clip art and hooked by Sandy England, Toronto, Ontario, Canada, 2015. MARK GUILBEAUL

Sandy England
Toronto, Ontario, Canada

Sandy began hooking around 1973 and paused from 1991 to 2008, when she retired and returned to the fold. She is now a member of RHGNS, ATHA, and TIGHR, and she sits on the board of the OHCG. This is her first piece to be featured in Celebration; she feels very honored.

Very effective use of dip dyes and beading. Lovely balance of colors; precise shading moves your eye around the piece. Beautifully colored, with great attention to detail and placement.

Young Girl Writing

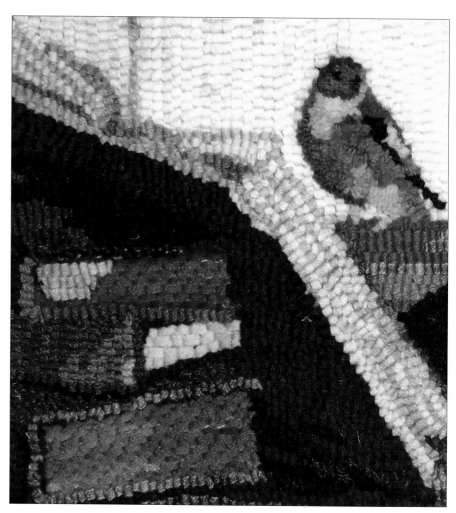

Since 2004, when rug hooking became a regular part of my life, I have endeavored each year to take a class in order to focus on a subject or technique that would expand my horizons. In 2014, the Rug Hooking Guild of Nova Scotia Rug School offered a class with Anne Lockhart to explore the Masters. With this subject in mind, I spent many hours searching the Internet, saving images that appealed to me.

Young Girl Writing was one of several images chosen, and oddly enough, painted by an artist of whom I had never heard. This prompted me to do a little research into Sophie de Bouteiller (pseudonym Henriette Browne). I have found that research adds significantly to the enjoyment of hooking; it is an opportunity to learn a little about history and appreciate what has gone before us.

Following the decision to hook this masterpiece, I searched for the best-quality image I could find for details and colors. Some versions were duller and looked more blue or gray, but I wanted something bright. Many Masters paintings are dark, something that does not appeal to me and my wools.

With a picture in hand, I rummaged through my stash to find suitable colors. I also sent a note to my instructor, Anne, so she would be aware of my choice ahead of time. To that time, I had only done a Santa face and a self-portrait using skin-tone swatches, so I was surprised to receive a note from Anne suggesting the face could be hooked nicely with a dip-dyed wool. Putting swatches away, I dyed three pieces of wool, finally achieving a color that appealed to me. It made hooking the face very easy, and the effect was lovely.

The largest area in this mat is the background wall, and there was nothing in my stash to suit. So I dyed wool for the background, along with a few smaller pieces for specific areas.

The biggest challenge for me was the blouse—how to keep it light enough against the background, and how to achieve the look of old cotton with all its wrinkles. A line of fine yarn hooked between the wool loops sharpened the edge perfectly.

Perhaps the most trying area was the bird cage; it was worked and reworked so that the bird was not lost, the cage kept its 3-D look, and the millet was faintly visible. I like to enhance a mat with special techniques, so the brighter bird is slightly sculpted and the pages in the books are reverse-hooked.

G. Dianne Warren
St. John's, Newfoundland and Labrador, Canada

My first attempt to hook was in 1976: a challenge with a Chéticamp trivet kit, a little handmade hook, and basic instructions. Around 1990 I bought a Moshimer hook and finally finished the trivet. After retiring from a career in computer systems in 2004, I finally found the time, encouragement, and opportunity to take a class with the Rug Hooking Guild of Newfoundland and Labrador.

Young Girl Writing, 29" x 23", #3- and 4-cut hand-dyed and as-is wool on linen. Adapted from a painting by Henriette Browne and hooked by G. Dianne Warren, St. John's, Newfoundland and Labrador, Canada, 2015.

Flesh tones are luminous; particularly good use of fancy "stitches" to provide subtle variations in the books. I want to reach out and turn a page! Many brilliant elements: books, hands, blouse, bird cage, hair. Much detail, but also serenity.

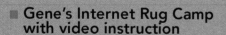

1875 Ship at Sea

"Twenty years from now, you will be more disappointed by the things that you didn't do than by the ones you did do. So throw off the bowlines. Sail away from the safe harbor. Catch the trade winds in your sails. Explore, Dream, Discover." — Mark Twain

My *1875 Ship at Sea* rug is dedicated to the memory of my brother Robert. Robert loved sailing and dreamed of building his own boat someday. Unfortunately, he passed away in 2007. Many of his years of service in the US Air Force were spent overseas in Germany, England, and Scotland. In Scotland he learned that the wool used to make Harris Tweed woolens came from flocks reared on the mainland of Scotland and that all Harris Tweed must be, by law, hand woven on a treadle loom by a weaver in the weaver's own home.

While in England, Robert commis-sioned a tailor to make two custom Harris Tweed wool sport coats. My brother was not accustomed to such luxury and treasured the opportunity to acquire such quality clothing produced through the proud craftsmanship of the weavers of Scotland. Years later, when the sport coats no longer fit him, Robert would not allow his wife to dispose of them. After his passing, my sister-in-law—knowing my love of rug hooking—offered the sport coats to me. At that point, I knew I would "build" that sailing vessel my brother had always dreamed of.

For some time, I had admired the *1875 Ship at Sea* pattern offered by Sally Kallin, of Pine Island Primitives. I ordered the smallest of her three patterns, while making sure I had adequate linen to include wording from the Mark Twain quote above. That quote provided inspiration for the rug design as well as serving as a reminder to actually "do."

I deconstructed the sport coats and dyed some of the wool with PRO Chem Teal. All the wool used in this rug is 100 percent wool and either dyed or used "as-is." Antique paisley was used in the creation of the flowers. I finished the rug with Pater-nayan and Waverly yarns. To pay tribute to Robert's military service, I chose to use Polly Minick's American-flag rug binding tape, to which I applied a wash to give a more primitive appearance.

I thoroughly enjoyed hooking this rug. I found that the size and weight of the rug presented its challenges during hooking and finishing. I am honored that this rug was chosen as a finalist. I believe my brother would have been impressed with this rug—although I am not sure he would have for-given me for cutting up his beloved Harris Tweed sport coats!

Diane Anderson
Bristol, Wisconsin

In 1987, a friend urged me to join Joyce Krueger's rug hooking class—a decision I do not regret. Rug hooking is my relaxation and occasionally, my therapy! This is my first rug chosen as a Celebration finalist.

In The Judges' Eyes

Lettering is skillfully done and a beautiful enhancement to the rug; stands out but does not take away. All the elements—ship, flowers, houses—work well together.

1875 Ship at Sea, 55½" x 32", #6-, 8-, 8.5-, and 9-cut wool on linen.
Designed by Sally Kallin and hooked by Diane Anderson, Bristol, Wisconsin, 2015. ARTS CAMERA PLUS

Homage to Humboldt

My fascination with natural history illustrations from the era before photography was the inspiration for this piece. Illustrators of that period often lacked the opportunity to observe living subjects in their actual environment. Employing a bit of creative license in the absence of accurate information, artists sometimes portrayed animals in fanciful poses and exotic settings.

The title *Homage to Humboldt* pays respect to the German naturalist and ecological visionary Alexander von Humboldt (1769-1859), one of the first to recognize the complexities and interconnectedness of the natural world. The father of modern environmentalism, he was regarded as the preeminent scientist of his time. Humboldt warned of the negative and potentially catastrophic impact of our destructive actions on nature.

As a graphic designer by profession, I am interested in the significance of symbols to human interaction. The snake is a powerful symbol—both positive and negative—in many cultures around the world. The snake in my piece (besides being a pleasing shape and a vehicle for pattern) represents danger, as it appears to be ready to strike at the fleeing bird. My aim was to create tension by freezing the action at the moment where it is unclear whether the bird will escape or be brought down by the snake. We are now witness to the repercussions of environmental abuse Humboldt warned of two centuries ago. There is realization of an uncertain future: as the bird, will our species escape the dangers of an altered climate or be consumed by the "snake"?

Beyond symbolism and storytelling, this piece was an opportunity to indulge my passion for pattern, shape, and color. I am a slow hooker, but the tactile and sensuous pleasures of working with wool compensate for the hours spent. The graphic art quality of rug hooking makes it a natural extension of my work as a designer. I begin with rough graphite sketches to work through ideas, then switch to colored pencils to refine layout and develop color. While hooking, the finished drawing serves as reference—although I frequently modify colors and shapes as the piece develops, sometimes reworking an area many times before I am satisfied. It is this immediate flexibility that makes rug hooking so appealing as a medium for artistic expression—technique does not dominate or inhibit the creative process.

Marilyn J. Motsch
Louisville, Kentucky

I hooked my first rug in 2005, drawing on skills and experience as a graphic designer and applying them to rug hooking. My love for anything related to textiles increasingly dominates my creative energies. Other "fibery" passions include knitting, knitwear design, spinning, and dyeing.

Homage to Humboldt, 18¾" x 20", #4- to 6-cut hand-dyed and as-is wool on linen.
Designed and hooked by Marilyn J. Motsch, Louisville, Kentucky, 2015.

Wonderful use of color; beautifully hooked; nice movement and flow of the design.

Hudson Valley Sheep

When I walked into the hooking room at The Star of Texas rug camp in Tyler, I was awe-struck by an absolutely beautiful rug. I knew immediately that I needed to hook that rug. The rug was *Hudson Valley Sheep* hooked by Jayne Hester. Since Jayne would be teaching the next year, I signed up for her class in order to avail myself of her expertise in color planning primitive designs with colors that are close in value.

Jayne helped guide me in selecting textured wools in muted colors that would nevertheless provide impact despite their low contrast. In class, I was able to work on only a few areas. With some great wool and informative notes in hand, I went home ready for a challenge.

Coming from the Gulf Coast, I was not familiar with how the valley should look, so I studied pictures of the Hudson Valley to try to gain a feel for the valley's color palette.

Hooking the river was the hardest part of the rug. There were two problems to tackle with the river: perspective and contrast. The river needed to look like it was flowing down into the valley and still provide a contrasting background for the sheep. A textured plaid was selected to achieve the effects for contrast. With that one plaid, I was able to "fussy-cut" it so that I had darks for the water flowing down the hill and to shade the sheep. Another part of the plaid provided the light for the tumbling water around the rocks.

The contrast between the light and dark sheep as well as variety in the size of the sheep provides the initial impact to draw you into the rug. The cascading river leads your eye into the middle of the scene. The large, dark tree dominates the area and is showcased by the soft contrast of the hills

and muted sky in the background.

I hooked several areas with different wools until I obtained the exact look I wanted. I snapped gray-scale pictures of the rug in progress to aid in judging contrast of the wools selected. I did integrate a mottled over-dyed texture for the large hill.

I have taken classes from some great teachers. Each has provided some knowledge to help create wonderful rugs that have now been in *Celebration* twice.

Cora Maldonado
Texas City, Texas

I have been hooking seriously for about 10 years. During that time, I have hooked approximately 40 rugs and mats. Mostly, I enjoy hooking in the primitive style. Thanks to Cynthia Norwood for starting my rug-hooking journey.

Hudson Valley Sheep, 33" x 41", #8.5 to 9-cut as-is and over-dyed textured wool on linen.
Designed by Bill Laraway and Carol Endres and hooked by Cora Maldonado, Texas City, Texas, 2014. BELINDA CANALES

Quilt Sampler for Wide Cut

I love traditional quilt patterns, but my old arthritic hands no longer can stand up to the grasping and pulling of a needle. And happily, I find rug hooking much more satisfying anyway.

I drew some of my favorite quilt block patterns on individual squares of copier paper and moved them around to balance the design and to move selected colors around the rug. A year later the pattern—squares taped together—still sat ignored in the closet. I drew it out on nice, clean rolled paper and gave it to Charlotte Price, owner of the House of Price pattern company. A couple of years after that, I had finished a bunch of smallish projects—mostly for Southern McGown Teachers Workshop and guild challenges—and decided it was time to hook a bigger rug. I was, after all, a rug hooker, not a hot pad hooker.

Charlotte had my Quilt Sampler pattern on bleached linen, but even after I received it, I let more months pass. In 2015, instructor Anne Bond emailed to ask what my project would be at the Ohio Rug Camp. I had put together a few stacks of wool that were the colors of our master bathroom, and I also sent Anne a drawing of the pattern.

When I got to rug camp, Anne had colored the sketch with my colors. I needed purple for the sashing, she said, and I might as well outline the motifs with the same dark purple in a narrower cut. She had overdyed some Dorr black with her Paw Paw Purple formula—a stroke of genius. She suggested I hook the light backgrounds using a higgledy-piggledy technique in a #6 cut to further differentiate the backgrounds from the motifs. I had dyed several pieces of textured wool with Majic Carpet orange and more pieces with Susan Feller's fraktur gold. The rest of the wools were as-is textures.

I hooked happily for three months, figuring out each square as if it was a puzzle all its own. I hooked most of the backgrounds as I went along. I dyed more dark Paw Paw Purple and used it for the show binding, cutting three-inch-wide pieces of wool to cover the linen that I rolled forward and stitched for self-cording. It is a perfect match—though the dog hair does seem to catch and show on Paw Paw Purple.

Fritz Mitnick
Pittsburgh, Pennsylvania

Fritz Mitnick is an active McGown Certified Instructor who teaches in her home, at community facilities, and at workshops and camps. Currently ATHA Region 6 representative, she has been hooking for 19 years and still learns from every teacher. Many of her patterns are available for purchase from Honey Bee Hive.

Quilt Sampler for Wide Cut, 32½" x 53", #6- to 8-cut hand-dyed, overdyed, and as-is textured wool on linen. Designed and hooked by Fritz Mitnick, Pittsburgh, Pennsylvania, 2015. ALAN J. KING

The Gift Is Small, The Love Is Great

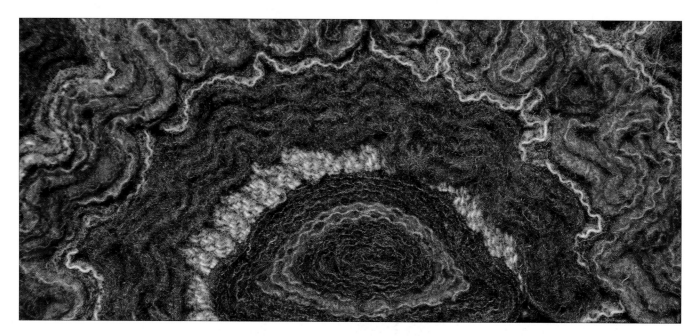

The Gift Is Small, The Love Is Great is a pattern that spoke to me as soon as I saw it. The distelfink in Pennsylvania Dutch art symbolizes happiness and good fortune. Just looking at this design made me smile.

The distelfink birds drew my attention first. There is a great deal of charm in the simplicity of the large motifs, yet within each shape there are so many places to add color. It was important to make each bird different in its own way. Keeping the color balanced was a challenge. This is a Barbara Carroll design from a coverlet pattern. She reminded me as she helped plan this project that the color change had to be subtle so as not to distract from the whole concept. I used both dyed and as-is wool. This rug was hooked on primitive linen with #8.5-cut strips of wool, but I do not hesitate to use more than one size cut of wool within a rug if it is necessary and adds interest.

I feel that the simplicity of design in primitive work is beautiful. In primitive rugs—where the figures are bold and often abstract—strength is added to the design using wider strips and more textured wool. Texture adds visual variety and movement to a rug. Wider strips of wool show more texture much like a Van Gogh painting, where each stroke of paint shows the hand of the artist. Working with textured wool and a wider cut allows me to create more freely. For me, rug hooking has been a medium that encourages learning and experimenting.

The most time consuming and difficult part of this rug was the bottom. I thought it was interesting having a border only at the bottom but wanted to give a touch of fun and added interest. This seemed to be the perfect place to use some techniques I had learned from Ali Strebel. After some experimenting with different methods, I decided that shirring and coiling was the answer. It worked beautifully. The Gift Is Small, The Love Is Great won a commendation for best primitive rug from the Brandywine Rug Hooking Guild at their Autumn Hook-in.

For me, designing patterns and creating hooked rugs has opened an interesting venue of possibilities as an artist and lover of textiles. I love rug hooking—but more important are the friends I have made while on this journey.

Joanne Gerwig
Freeland, Maryland

Joanne Gerwig is the owner of Woodcrest Rug Designs. She has been designing and hooking rugs for about 12 years. This is Joanne's third appearance in Celebration. *Joanne is a member of Mason Dixon ATHA and The Brandywine Rug Hooking Guild. She is a classically trained professional artist and works out of her studio in Freeland.*

In The Judges' Eyes

Stunning, exciting color choices and lovely textures; fun and inventive use of standing wool in the area at the bottom.

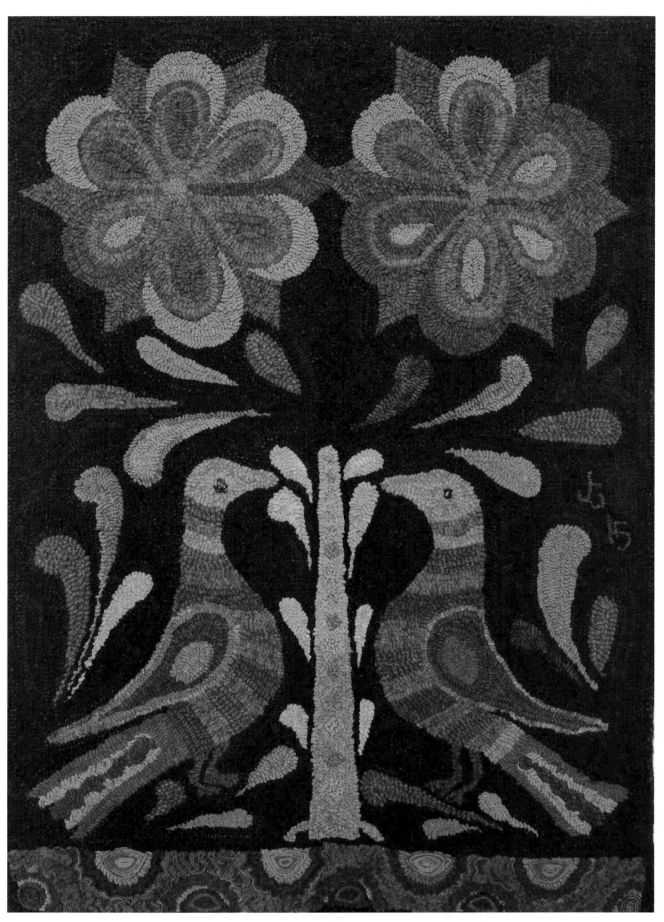

The Gift Is Small, The Love Is Great, 34" x 47", #8.5 hand-dyed and as-is wool on linen.
Designed by Barbara Carroll and hooked by Joanne Gerwig, Freeland, Maryland, 2015. TOM GETZ

The Old Barn

I grew up on a small farm near St. Paul, Minnesota, with two brothers and two sisters. Some wonderful memories are associated with the old barn on the family farm: building forts with secret tunnels in the hay bales, playing hide and seek, and jumping off the barn roof into a snow drift in the winter. I wanted to create a barn that would bring back those childhood memories.

After designing *The Old Barn*, I contacted Cathy Stephan, who was going to be my instructor at the Arrowhead Hookcrafters Rug School, to help color plan the rug. The primary focus was to create a red barn that looked rustic and weathered. Cathy dyed my barn wool with a dye she calls her "garbage" dye. Cathy saves her leftover dyes in a jug,

with the result that the mixture turns out to be a dull, dusty red. This red dye was used to overdye a variety of wool I had for the barn boards. To make the barn boards look even more weathered, I cut some very narrow strips of dark wool and worked these strips randomly between the boards.

I divided the sky wool into three values. The darkest value of wool was hooked at the top of the sky, with the bottom of the sky the lightest value. The remainder of the wool filled in the middle. Using the lightest value of wool next to the mountains provided the needed contrast between the sky and mountains. The mountains were hooked with four different wools, both overdyed and off-the-bolt.

The foliage on the tree was hooked with leftover wool from the barn and worms from previously hooked rugs. By hooking a small number of loops of different wools for the canopy, I was able to create a tree that was at its peak fall color.

The background around the barn was wool from off the bolt. Cathy and I decided to keep the field around the barn subdued to complement the weathered barn look. I had some as-is wool that was a value darker than the field. This I used to provide some subtle shadows by the fence and tree.

My goal with *The Old Barn* rug was to create an old-looking, weathered, and rustic barn within an overall old-looking rug. I am very pleased with the result.

Jacqueline A. Albrecht
Hastings, Minnesota

I began rug hooking in 2006 with the Hastings Rug Hookers. Over the past 10 years I have attended many rug hooking camps and workshops. My philosophy is to learn something new from each instructor and incorporate this information in my future rugs. My favorite part of rug hooking is the color planning of the rug.

In The Judges' Eyes

Charming! Nice use of textures and directional hooking; good use of color to create the illusion of space.

The Old Barn, 36" x 27", #8 hand-cut overdyed and as-is wool on linen.
Designed and hooked by Jacqueline A. Albrecht, Hastings, Minnesota, 2015. LYNN JOHNSON

Zig Zag Primitive

There is nothing like adding some vintage wools to a primitive rug design. They may not be new and perfect, but their addition puts me in that primitive working mode, which is often so hard to get your mind channeled into.

We naturally like to be neat and produce a neat, attractive rug. It can be difficult to just hook wool in and not take out . . . to incorporate odd shapes, or add out-of-place colors in background areas.

This rug came about—as some of mine do—by putting together a rug from a hodge-podge of notes, bits of photos, and random inspirations. If I see something that intrigues me, I will write it down for possible later use. In this case a "pot shaped like a tooth" was what caught my eye in an antique store: A flower pot needs to be filled. A photo of electric peacock blue with outrageous oranges piqued my interest: What if they were muted a bit? My design was too neat, so I added a quick sketch of a cat and bird below the pot. They have no relation to the pot of flowers, which adds a naïve touch. Since I didn't want more color and clutter, I eliminated leaves, and—wanting a frame—I simply drew a wavy "zig zag" line around the outer edge.

Then, off to my stash of wools to select quite a pile of both textured and "solids" to play with—mostly dyed, as that is my pref-erence. They were then piled up and moved about to eliminate any that bothered my eye. Some chosen pieces I really liked were just small pieces, and when they were used up I didn't try to find a match. Wools were cut either #7 or #8, and I also used any strips that were a bit smaller or larger.

Then I just hooked—and had a great time loving the freedom of it all. What went in, stayed in. I did pay attention to color balance, as the lack of it bothers me.

There is also a secret message (a concept developed by Bev Conway) visible only on the back of this rug, which states,"It is what it is." In this case, "it" is very primitive!

Jeanne Benjamin
Brookfield, Massachusetts
Jeanne learned to hook in 1971 and became a McGown Certified Instructor in 1979. She is a traveling teacher at several events yearly. Jeanne owns New Earth Designs/Lib Callaway Patterns, and is known for her color planning and variety of dyed wools.

In The Judges' Eyes

Refreshing bold color choices; well executed and delightful; captures the spirit and feeling of the old antique rugs we love. Design creates sense of excitement; love the panache of this hooker.

Zig Zag Primitive, 35" x 43", #7- and 8-cut hand-dyed, mostly vintage wool.
Designed and hooked by Jeanne Benjamin, Brookfield, Massachusetts, 2015.

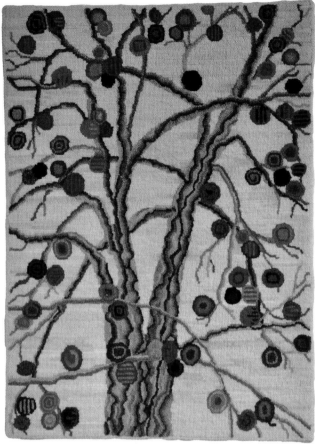

December Apples, 18½" x 25", #4-cut, hand-dyed wool on rug warp. Designed and hooked by Lil Quanz, Baden, Ontario, Canada, 2015. KATE QUANZ

World on a String, approximately 11" diameter, #4-, 6-, and hand-cut wool on monk's cloth. Adapted and hooked by Brigitta Phy, Sebastopol, California, 2015. BRUCE SHIPPEE

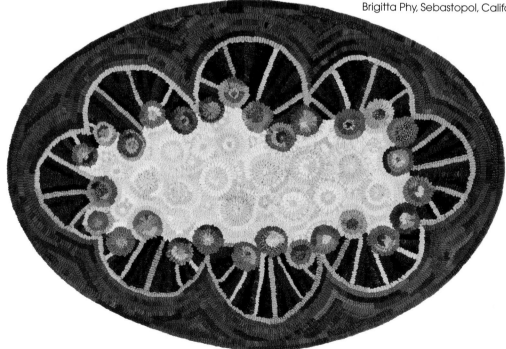

Doily Oval Rug, 36" x 25", #9- to 9½-cut new and recycled wool. Designed by Michele Micarelli and hooked by Sheri J. Bennett, Chattanooga, Tennessee, 2014. JESSE LANGSTON

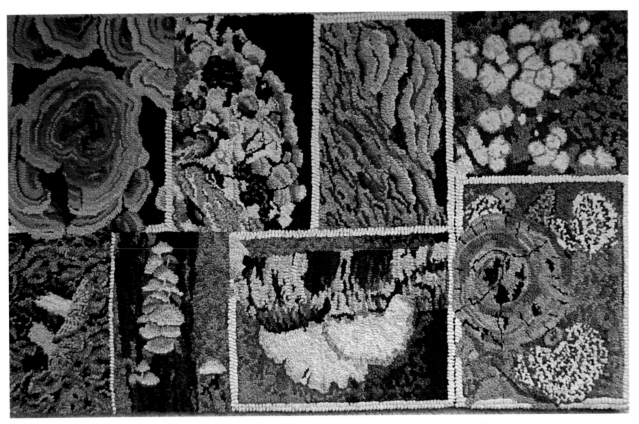

Fungi II, 28½" x 17½", #2- to 5-cut hand-dyed and as-is wool on monk's cloth.
Designed and hooked by Lyle E. Drier, Waukesha, Wisconsin, 2015. DENNIS DRIER

Klimtomanie, 48" x 30", #3- to 9-cut hand-dyed wool, sari silk, specialty yarn, and quillies on linen. Adapted from works
by Gustav Klimt and hooked by Felicia Mennin, New York, New York, 2015. CYNTHIA MACMILLAN

Magnolia, 28" x 47", #3- and 4-cut hand-dyed wool and ribbon on linen. Designed by Harry M. Fraser Company and hooked by Val M. Carter, Springfield, Virginia, 2015.

October, December & June, 14" x 49", #3-cut hand-dyed wool and silk on linen. Designed and hooked by Tammy B. Godwin, Louisville, Kentucky, 2015.

Paisley Mix-up, 60" x 39½", #3- to 8-cut hand-dyed and as-is wool.
Designed and hooked by Judy Quintman, Wilmington, North Carolina, 2014. IMPACT XPOZURES

The Ever-Changing Landscape of Colour Renewed, 4' x 3', #3- to #8-cut hand-dyed and as-is wool on linen. Designed and hooked by Christine D. Hornby, Grand Haven, Michigan, 2015.

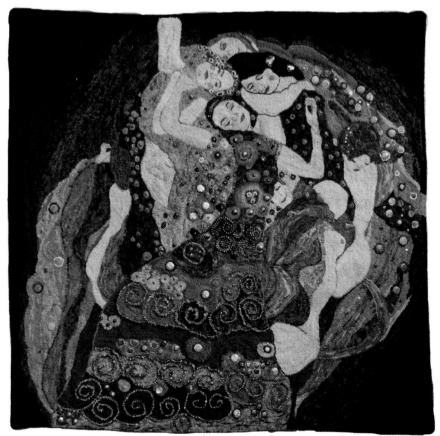

The Virgin, 40" x 41", #1- to 6-cut wool and semi-precious gemstones on monk's cloth. Adapted from a painting by Gustav Klimt and hooked by Cindy Irwin, Lancaster, Pennsylvania, 2015. DEB BURSTEN

Who Lives There?, 38½" x 29", 3-ply hand-dyed wool yarn, 4-ply wool yarn, hand-cut wool strips, and polymer clay embellishments on monk's cloth. Designed and hooked by Simone Vojvodin, Parkhill, Ontario, Canada, 2015.

Syrian Fragment of Floor Mosaic (circa 526-540),
17" x 32", #4- to 6-cut wool on linen. Adapted and hooked by
Timmie Wiant, St. Louis, Missouri, 2014. PAUL HEIDBREIDER

The Lovers, 24" x 42½", #2- to 8-cut wool on linen. Adapted
from Tarot card images and hooked by Elizabeth B. Marino,
South Egremont, Massachusetts, 2015. JANE MCWHORTER

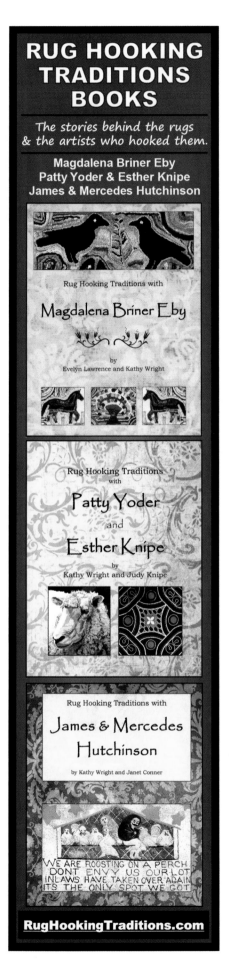